Deliver Me From

Talking Too Much

The Spiritual Significance of Moving In Silence

Protecting Your Dreams from The Enemy's Devices, Being Patient with God's Timing and Trusting His Divine Plan for Your Life

*Initially Released Title: The Quiet Power Of Moving In Silence

By Lynn R. Davis

PUBLISHED BY: LYNN R DAVIS, *Author of Deliver Me From Negative Self-Talk*

COPYRIGHT © 2024

TABLE OF CONTENTS

A wise man once said absolutely nothing at all.

-unknown

Introduction

This book might be for you if:

- You constantly find yourself oversharing.
- You tend to tell too much personal information.
- Your confidence has been betrayed.
- You feel like no one *really* supports your dreams.
- You have a Joseph dream but don't know what to do next.

Don't be like me, and learn the hard way, why you shouldn't trust everyone blindly without using discernment. I believe discernment is what our grandparents were talking about when they said, "You ain't got the sense God gave you."

The sense God gave us is our spiritual discernment. The ability to know something in our gut, soul, and spirit, without an ounce of physical evidence. It's a knowing.

If there is one thing I have learned in my 50-plus years of living as a Christian, it's this: talking too much will get you into a whole heap of trouble. Keep your plans, goals, visions, and dreams to yourself. Allow them the opportunity to take root and develop before exposing them to external influences over which you have no control. I promise you that this will increase your chances of success, as your endeavors are shielded from early interference.

I pray that whoever you are, you find this message and receive it as confirmation that God needs you to move in silence during this next season of your life.

For others, if you're holding this book, you may have had the unfortunate experience of sharing something personal with the wrong person, and doing so blew up in your face. I'm truly sorry you went through that, and I hope this message brings encouragement. God is mindful of you. Things are working in your favor.

Most of us have been there. I know I have. This message is for me as much as it is for you, the reader. In a time where oversharing is encouraged, we must be careful that we aren't boundaryless to the point of our detriment. Learning to move in silence gives us an added layer of protection from the craftiness of sabotaging enemies, human and spiritual- "the pestilence that walketh in darkness" and "destruction that wasted at noonday". Psalm 91:6

Our dreams, opportunities, and accomplishments are gifts from God that must be valued and protected. You would never take your most prized possession outside and place it on a busy sidewalk. It would be stolen, mishandled, or worse destroyed. You should never share anything valuable with someone who would not value it or being possessed by a spirit of greed, would try to steal, kill, or destroy it.

Keep your plans private, whether your plans involve a new job, financial venture, or personal relationship.

7 RISKS OF OVERSHARING

1. Disrupted peace. You lose the necessary time for rest and reflection.
2. Unnecessary distractions. New opportunities and plans can be intercepted or disrupted.
3. Added competition. You subject your goals and aspirations to undercover rivals.
4. Overexposure and vulnerability. Opening yourself to judgment and scrutiny.
5. Increased anxiety and stress. Worrying about others' opinions and reactions.
6. Misunderstandings. People twist your words or question your intentions.
7. Confusion and chaos. Operating with clouded thinking and a lack of discernment.

Reading and understanding this message will help you become more aware of the people around you as well as the unseen spiritual influences. These invisible forces can be just as challenging—if not more so—than the people you interact with daily.

By the time you finish this book, I hope you will understand:

- Why you should have more discretion when it comes to your business, dreams, and goals,
- Why it is in your best interest to sometimes keep your business to yourself- at least in the beginning,
- When to employ solitude versus the use of isolation,
- And how you can use moving in silence as your secret weapon- both spiritually and physically.

He who has ears, let them hear. *Matthew 11:15*

Years ago, a newlywed couple told me a story. Shortly after their wedding, they were eager to buy a charming little cottage that had just hit the market.

Thrilled about the opportunity, they shared their plans with close friends and family during a gathering.

The following week, they met with the seller, only to discover that their family member had also contacted the seller and expressed interest in the property.

The news shocked the couple—they couldn't believe a relative would compete for the same house. Feeling hurt and betrayed, they decided to withdraw their offer.

Ironically, the family member who attempted to intervene couldn't qualify financially, so neither party ended up purchasing the home. From this experience, the couple learned a powerful lesson about the importance of moving in silence.

This book is in your hands for a reason. There is something that God is leading you to pursue- a dream or goal that He wants you to accomplish. If the message of moving in silence keeps appearing, it's no coincidence.

Trust that God is prompting you to act with wisdom, strategy, and discretion. Use discernment from this day forward. The Holy Spirit is ready to guide you when you are ready to be led. Let's get into it.

"There is a time to tear and a time to mend. A time to keep silent, and a time to speak." - Ecclesiastes 3:7

MEMORY VERSE: PROVERBS 17: 28

Even fools are thought to be wise if they keep silent and discerning if they hold their tongues.

PRAYER

Heavenly Father, grant me the wisdom to guard my tongue and the discipline to remain quiet when needed. Teach me to speak with discernment and to honor You in all my communications and actions. In Jesus' name, Amen.

AFFIRMATION

I exercise wisdom by holding my tongue and practicing discernment. My words reflect thoughtfulness and honor to God.

MANTRA

"Silence reveals wisdom; discernment guides my words."

CHAPTER 1

STOP TELLING EVERYBODY YOUR BUSINESS

Welcome to the first day of *Keeping People Out Of Your Business 101.* **In this class, you will** learn the basics of moving in silence: why moving in silence is so important, how to navigate friends and family, how to identify unseen enemies, how to protect your dreams, and more.

Moving in silence is **a** skill that can benefit us all from the womb to the grave. "Before I formed you in the womb, I knew you". There was a plan from the beginning. Your mission is to understand and execute God's plan. The enemy's mission is to steal, kill, and destroy it.

"…. until you can discern between those who wish to pat you on the back and those who dream of stabbing you in it- it's best to move in silence."

The fewer people you tell your business, the slimmer the chance for an enemy to spoil your plans. There's a saying, "Too many cooks in the kitchen spoil the broth."

Moving in silence has many moving parts, mental, physical, emotional, and spiritual. We will talk about them. First, let's discuss moving in silence amongst our inner circle, close family, and friends.

This is a difficult subject if you are accustomed to sharing every detail of your life with every member of your inner circle. It will be an adjustment not only for you but for them as well.

MOVING IN SILENCE BEGINS AT HOME

Joseph dreamed that he would become a great ruler. In his dream, his family bowed before him. Joseph shared his dream with his brothers, and they hated him for it. Driven by jealousy and animosity, they sold Joseph into slavery and lied to their father about what they had done. People will hurt you and then lie about what they did. Joseph's story has many messages, which I will share throughout this guide, but the first is this, not everyone, even those closest to you, will celebrate your dreams.

"...deep down they know that you have the potential to become exactly what you are dreaming of and the very idea of you succeeding beyond them irritates their demons."

Joseph shared a dream. A movie in his mind that hadn't even come to fruition yet. Still, just his dream alone was enough to anger the people who heard it. Whether you notice it or not, your dreams fill some people with madness. But why? One reason could be they do not yet have a dream of their own. This makes them feel insecure or jealous.

What they fail to realize is that God blesses us through people. You have a heart for God and He could easily use you to bless them just as Joseph was used to bless his family in the end. But I'm getting ahead of myself. By attacking you, they are essentially attacking themselves and potentially blocking blessings that could have been funneled through you.

This is not to say that people need you to receive a blessing. Don't take it that far. Just understand that God uses whomever he chooses. And sometimes the people we least expect are chosen for His purposes.

Another reason your dreams anger people is for lack of faith. They cannot fathom your dream coming true because they walk by sight and not by faith.

Thirdly, fear causes some people to believe that you will leave them behind. They would rather you not succeed at all if it means you will leave them behind or elevate above them.

Whether they know it or not, deep down they do not have your best interest at heart. They hold secret animosity and envy.

Some of them even see your greatness before you do. They know, if you dream it, you have the potential to achieve it.

For them, the very idea of you succeeding beyond them irritates their unhealed soul.

Like Joseph's brothers, there are people around you who will be annoyed by your audacity to dream, let alone talk about it. This is why, in the beginning, it is wiser to keep the business of your dreams to yourself.

"If your dreams and goals drive them crazy, imagine what your success will do."

Keeping it all balanced, every family experiences disagreements, and you should reconcile whenever possible. A loving family is a blessing and should never be taken for granted. Disagreements between members of this nature are not the subject here. So don't read this and create a problem where there isn't one. Just tuck this information in your back pocket in case you need it later.

This chapter applies to people in your circle who **you know** operate from a mean-spirited energy. Repeatedly, they have proven their disloyalty.

Yet, you continue to trust them with your dreams, aspirations, and personal details of your life. Only to feel slighted, overlooked, or worse sabotaged.

These people family or not, cannot and should not be trusted with the personal details of your life, let alone your God-given dreams and aspirations.

"Here comes that dreamer!" they said to each other. "Come now, let's kill him and throw him into one of these cisterns and say that a ferocious animal devoured him." Genesis 37

They could be talking about you before you even enter the room. Many times, we assume that family is synonymous with loyalty, but that is not always so.

Joseph was so busy seeking validation from his family that he didn't realize his dreams were irritating their demons.

Pursuing your dreams and goals without relying on validation from family and close friends will be difficult at first, because you may be in the habit of oversharing or people-pleasing.

Moving in silence exhibits self-reliance and confidence. The more you learn to rely on the guidance of the Holy Spirit, the less you will depend on the approval of others.

Your self-confidence will increase- without the overshadowing of other people's predicted outcomes. Soon you won't need validation from anyone. Just because people in your circle don't see your gift as a blessing or appreciate them, doesn't mean you should give up.

The gift Joseph's family despised him for is the very gift that elevated him. You may be the black sheep of your family, but no matter, there is another group who will be blessed by the gift God gave you.

"Because of Joseph, the LORD began to bless Potiphar's family and field." -Genesis 39:5

So don't feel like you need to win over the doubters. Your gift will speak for itself in due season. At the right time, your work will be revealed and people who witness the revelation will speak.

Proverbs 27:2 says, "Let another praise you, and not your own mouth; a stranger, and not your own lips."

Sometimes a stranger will sing your
praises faster than the people in your
circle.

Potiphar recognized Joseph's dreams as a gift and elevated him unlike some of his own family who resented his dreams and betrayed him. Navigating family requires delicacy and patience. "…the dream God has given you is for a bigger purpose than to impress the people in your household. Sometimes your gift is meant to bless households around the world."

Only God knows what you are here to do. "Before He formed you in the womb, He knew you". People who are not led by the Holy Spirit will not be able to discern your gifts and calling.

They will make judgments and assumptions from their own limited points of view. That may be their role to play in your life because sometimes betrayal will light a fire in our soul and fuel us to push forward.

Spare yourself from being thrown in the pit by moving in silence. Had Joseph moved in silence, perhaps the story would have played out a different way. Maybe he didn't have to be thrown in a pit, sold into slavery, and put in jail. Perhaps his gifts could have evolved naturally. He could have met Potiphar under different circumstances and still elevated and helped his family through the famine.

I say this to say, whether you move in silence or plaster your business on social media, God can still silence the enemy and get you to where you need to be. But wouldn't you rather just avoid all the drama and move in silence?

Jesus said, "Father, forgive them, for they do not know what they are doing." Luke 23:34

There are people who purposely try to destroy others. They operate in a steal, kill, and destroy energy.

In the case of Joseph's siblings, they knew exactly what they were doing. Still, in the end, Joseph forgave them. This lesson of forgiveness is powerful. Forgiveness frees you mentally, physically, and emotionally.

It's not easy, but it is necessary to move forward successfully. Otherwise, you are volunteering to carry an enormous amount of baggage on your journey. It's difficult to move in silence when there is a bag full of anger, resentment, and bitterness dragging behind you. Pass the test of forgiveness. It will release you from burdens.

Your dream was given to you, not the people around you. Some don't care to understand why you have the dreams that you have let alone what they mean. Your drive and ambition baffle them because they don't know the source of your power and strength. To them, you are just a dreamer who won't be quiet.

7 TIMES WHEN YOU MIGHT WANT TO CONSIDER MOVING IN SILENCE

1. Starting New Ventures. Protect your innovative ideas and projects from premature exposure.
2. Planning Long-Range Goals. Keep your plans to yourself!
3. Pursuing New Opportunities. Prevent others from undermining your efforts before you even get started.
4. Dealing With Legal Matters. Maintain integrity and avoid external influences that could sabotage the outcome.
5. Managing Financial Resources. Keep prying eyes out of your money matters.
6. Managing Stress and Anxiety: Address worries privately or with a professional to find solutions.
7. Learning New Skills or Pursuing New Goals: Focus on personal growth and development without distraction.

Always seek to forgive, but I never advise you to forget the lesson. Sometimes upon reflection, you will discern that a person was sincere.

Pray for them but continue to move in silence. Keep your dreams to yourself and keep your business matters private. These life lessons will make you much wiser and more discerning. Trust is earned and even then, that doesn't mean lower your guard completely.

After testing their intentions, Joseph forgave his brothers. Even though they betrayed him in the past, he had empathy and gave them another chance once he saw that they were sorry for their actions. Discern people's intentions and keep your own pure. This way, you protect yourself and your dream. Had Joseph sought revenge, he would have been no better than his brothers. "Vengeance is mine, says the Lord". When you forgive and continue to move with discretion, you call less attention to yourself and maintain control over your narrative.

Should someone have hidden intentions to shoot down your dreams, your silence will shield you from the stray bullets of schemes, plots, gossip, slander, and misunderstandings because the less they know, the better.

"Always celebrate someone else's accomplishments, even if you're going through a

> *tough time. If anything, celebrating someone else gives us inspiration."*

As you achieve milestones, move in silence and wait for the right timing. Ecclesiastes 3:1 reminds us, "To everything, there is a season and a time for every matter under heaven." Timing is everything. For example, it may be the wrong time to share your financial achievements with someone who just filed for bankruptcy or lost their job. Don't misunderstand this for dimming your light or lowering yourself to make someone else feel superior. I'm saying that compassion, common sense, and empathy go a long way, and we must learn to navigate situations with grace and wisdom. This shows emotional intelligence.

> *"To everything, there is a season and a time for every matter under heaven."*

Circumstances change from day to day, but not everyone is emotionally mature enough to navigate the ebb and flows of life. In healthy dynamics, our achievements will be celebrated regardless.

I will always celebrate someone else's accomplishments, even if I'm going through a tough time. Celebrating someone else inspires me. I haven't always been this way. In the early days, I'd ask, "God, when is it my turn?" As you grow and mature, you will understand, that "God is no respecter of persons". Though we may not have the same circumstances, we all have the same birthright as His children. The opportunity to overcome, progress, and succeed is available to us all. Some endure more than others, but they choose to go for it and they succeed against the odds. We all have the choice to at least try.

DREAMERS WALK A NARROW PATH

Moving in silence will not make you popular. Everyone won't understand or support your choice to move in silence. You may be labeled as antisocial or accused of thinking you are better than they are. That's part of the journey. As long as you walk in the spirit of love, you have nothing to feel bad about.

You won't win with some people no matter what you do, so do what the Holy Spirit leads you to and you will not go wrong. It will not always be easy, but it will be right.

Maintain a pure heart and set healthy boundaries. This at the minimum, is necessary to shield you from peer pressure and give you the strength to deal with adversity. Thank God for His protection and guidance.

In Psalm 91:4, it is written, "He will cover you with his feathers, and under his wings you will find refuge; his faithfulness will be your shield and rampart."

The Psalms remind us that even in difficult times, God's protection is a constant presence, providing safety and comfort. Trusting in His protective care allows us to navigate sticky relationship dynamics with confidence, knowing that He watches over us and shields us from dangers both seen and unseen.

Sharpening your discernment and praying for guidance when you are unsure will help you navigate the complexities of close relationships. Proverbs 3:5-6 advises, "Trust in the Lord with all your heart, and do not lean on your own understanding. In all your ways acknowledge Him, and He will direct your paths."

There are a lot of emotions involved when dealing with people in our close circles. Moving in silence must be done prayerfully and strategically with wisdom and love, but keeping it all balanced, everyone does not deserve a pass.

"When you do something to the least of them, you've done it to me." If you are being abused or bullied in any way, you need to seek help and strategically remove yourself. The most important love to exhibit in a case like this is self-love.

Your health, emotional, and physical well-being are the priority and the first step to taking your power back is speaking out and getting help.

"Emotional intelligence is the ability to acknowledge and understand your own emotions, as well as to recognize how you influence the emotions of others."

Move with discernment. Never fixate on retaliation or hold a grudge. Otherwise, you waste valuable time and energy, better spent pursuing your goals. Remove yourself or communicate your boundaries with love. Move forward knowing God is with you every step of the way.

If you move the way God instructs you, He will have your back. How do you know that you are being instructed to move away? Everyone's situation is different, so I can only tell you from my experience. If you are in a constant state of fear, worry, anxiety, and stress and your health is being negatively impacted- you need to at the very least, *consider* seeking wise counsel or putting distance between you and whatever or whoever is causing it. We've covered a lot of information about why you should move in silence and how discretion can be necessary even in our closest circles.

We will conclude this chapter with a very telling bible verse from Micah Chapter 7. Verse 5 reads, "Do not trust a neighbor; put no confidence in a friend. Even with the woman who lies in your embrace guard the words of your lips." Verse 6 continues, "For a son dishonors his father, a daughter rises up against her mother, a daughter-in-law against her mother-in-law— a man's enemies are the members of his own household". And verse 7 states, "But as for me, I watch in hope for the Lord, I wait for God my Savior; my God will hear me".

As you see from Micah, the enemy can use anyone to come against you. So before you can truly master moving in silence, you must understand the kinds of personalities that watch you, and why.

In the next chapter, we spend some time breaking down the types and characteristics of those people. Remember to cover yourself, your family, and your blessings in daily prayer. "Pray without ceasing." Read 1 Thessalonians 5:15-18.

Follow
your
DREAMS

MEMORY VERSE: JEREMIAH 1:5 (NIV)

"Before I formed you in the womb I knew you, before you were born, I set you apart; I appointed you as a prophet to the nations."

PRAYER

Heavenly Father, thank You for knowing me and setting me apart even before I was formed in the womb. Guide me to fulfill the purpose You have appointed for my life and grant me the courage to walk in obedience to Your calling. In Jesus' name. Amen.

AFFIRMATION

I am chosen, known, and set apart by God for a unique and divine purpose. I walk confidently in His plan for my life.

MANTRA

"Before I was formed, I was known by God and chosen."

CHAPTER 2

YOU CAN'T TELL EVERYBODY EVERYTHING

Rockwell had a hit in the 80's titled Somebody's Watching Me. The lyrics live rent-free in my head to this day. "I'm just an average guy, with an average life...I always feel like somebody's watching me."

If you feel like you are being watched, you're probably not paranoid, because people do pay attention, even when they pretend not to. Some mean well, some are just nosey, and unfortunately, a few have ill intentions. That's why it's essential to discern who deserves access to your plans and dreams and who doesn't.

We find another example of this in Joseph's story. He was serving in his master's house, minding his business, doing his job, like many of you. Little did he know that someone had eyes on him. His boss's wife watched Joseph with lust in her eyes.

"And it came to pass after these things, that his master's wife cast her eyes upon Joseph; and she said, Lie with me." Genesis 39:7

There are many people around you who watch your life. Some of them admire you, while others lust for your gifts among other things.

Your gifts will catch the attention of many people and for different reasons. To help describe the different personalities of these "watchers", I've created a few groups for discussion.

The characteristics of these silent watchers are based on analogies of church auxiliaries. Now before we go any further, understand that this is intended to be presented in a light-hearted tone and not taken literally. A good practice as you read about each personality is to consider how you might relate to these types, what lessons you can draw from them, and who you know that might fit their characteristics.

"The people who watch you have different agendas. Most are just nosey. Some will cheer you on. Some want what you have. Some want you to fail. Others haven't figured out which one they are yet."

GROUP ONE: THE CONGREGATION. They watch you because they need direction. The Congregation listens to what you say, watches how you move; and takes copious notes on your accomplishments and failures. They have ambitions, but they aren't sure how to proceed.

They need guidance and your life inspires them. So, they sit silently and observe your every move. They frequently gather with others from The Congregation to discuss your life, sometimes passing judgment. This group is secretly sizing you up to see if they want to become a member of your circle.

They are undercover copycats. They may mimic things about you that they like and gossip about things they don't. The Congregation will call or visit you from time to time to see what you have going on. They expect you to be loyal to them, but they are only loyal to themselves. They will show up only when it is convenient for them. On a more positive note, the Congregation can help you appreciate your purpose. This group also helps by reflecting on aspects of yourself that need growth. Watch them and learn what not to do. Learn to accept yourself and be authentic, stop judging, and embrace your uniqueness instead of mimicking others.

GROUP TWO: THE AMEN CORNER. These are the people who support you no matter what. You can do no wrong in their eyes. They are great supporters, but when you need someone to tell you the real hard truth, they don't have the heart to tell you anything other than what they think you want to hear.

They watch you and cheer you along your journey just the same. This group teaches us the value of giving and receiving constructive criticism and honest feedback. Ultimately, anyone who tells you what you want to hear is not helping you learn and grow. Likewise, we should be honest and compassionate with others as well.

GROUP THREE: THE PRAISE TEAM. These are the people who praise your accomplishments. When you do well, they praise you. When you need encouragement, they praise you. They are genuinely happy for you, but unlike the Amen Corner, they will let you know if your behavior is less than praiseworthy.

They don't praise nonsense like drama or mess. They watch you and offer praise when praise is warranted. This group teaches us to have integrity about what we praise and our expectations for receiving praise from others. We can learn to give praise where praise is due and offer correction and guidance in the appropriate seasons.

GROUP FOUR: THE CHOIR. These are people you are in harmony with. They are, or could someday become, your colleagues. This group is comprised of confident, charismatic, and influential comrades. They watch you with admiration and intrigue.

They've been where you are, and they recognize and respect your drive and determination. They might offer mentorship or collaboration. Whether you're experiencing a high or facing a low, the Choir personality will provide excellent backup to help you lead your success with confidence and effectiveness. This group teaches us the importance of embracing unity and harmony and uplifting others. They offer encouragement for others striving to reach their goals.

GROUP FIVE: THE PODIUM CHASERS. Be careful of this type. Your high energy, enthusiasm, and perceived success is attractive. They are the name-droppers and clout chasers. They lust for power and attention. They see your accomplishments as a train and want to stow away in your box car. In other words, they add no value and are just going along for the ride. It's not about what they can do for you, but all about how your success can benefit them. They like to be seen and heard.

Don't call them. They will call you- if you are deemed worthy. Allow this group to demonstrate the importance of integrity and reciprocity. Never take people for granted or use others for selfish purposes. Treat people with respect and set the expectation to be treated respectfully.

GROUP SIX: THE SOLICITORS. This group only comes around when they need something. They treat people as a means to an end. If you have a talent, skill, or resource that benefits them, they will befriend you, otherwise, you are of no consequence. It's especially important to move in silence around this group because they are always on the lookout for an opportunity to use someone else's accomplishments to their advantage.

They see your success, or lack thereof, as their gain. The Solicitors will find a way to capitalize on the people in their circle. If they cannot capitalize, they criticize and discard.

GROUP SEVEN: THE USHERS. This group knows everything about everyone. They keep a watchful eye and have no problem inserting themselves into other people's business offering unsolicited advice and direction. They can come across as overly assertive as they are very confident in their opinions and it's often their way or the highway. If you aren't careful, they will influence you to go in a direction you weren't planning, and you could end up someplace you don't want to be.

Ushers know the importance of seeing the big picture. They encourage us to think not only about where we want to go but also about where we *need* to be in the present moment. The Ushers teach us to be decisive about what we want to do and where we want to go.

They also teach us to make our own decisions and not follow the crowd. It's okay to take a different path. The Ushers also inspire us to have the courage to ask for directions when we feel lost.

GROUP EIGHT: THE **WELCOME COMMITTEE**. When this group sees you are trustworthy, authentic, and passionate about your vision, they will welcome you and be supportive. The welcome committee models hospitable behavior. They are good judges of character, but they do not stereotype or classify people based on status or material possessions. They are kind, generous, and genuine. Try to learn from them. Listen to their insights and share your own as well. Learn from them how to be kind and charitable to strangers.

GROUP NINE: THE MONITORING SPIRITS. There is more to life than we can physically see. Remember, we wrestle not against flesh and blood. As you pursue your dreams, you are observed by an invisible enemy who seeks to steal, kill, and destroy. These Monitoring Spirits can operate through any of the groups we mentioned before. For example, when The Congregation personality calls you under the guise of "checking in" on you, their real agenda, under the influence of a monitoring spirit, is to steal, kill, and destroy any aspiration that you share. Their only goal is to monitor your progress and sabotage it.

Monitoring spirits wage spiritual warfare on your dreams and goals. When you share your new project idea with a person operating as a monitoring spirit, you will notice out of nowhere, things start to go wrong.

Damages, accidents, illnesses, distractions, sudden repairs, you name it, all because you shared your business with a monitoring spirit who was assigned to steal, kill, and destroy. Thankfully, "the weapons of our warfare are not carnal, but mighty through God to the pulling down of strongholds".

LEARNING TO DISCERN

We must develop our ability to recognize the underlying intentions of others-especially dishonesty and deception. This is a skill crucial to effectively discerning your environment. Naiveté is not an option. Never take for granted that you know another person's intentions.

Take the time to get to know their character and personality without prejudging. Identify whether your values align. Don't make decisions strictly based on your emotions. Maintain clarity, objectivity, and rational thinking as much as humanly possible.

Be aware of deception and hidden motives. You must be vigilant and think critically, not taking things at face value. I believe these days it's known as, "keeping your head on a swivel", an expression for paying attention to your surroundings.

Learn to read the energy of the people in the room. What is their temperament? What does their body language tell you? How do you feel in their presence? What do you think about the conversation? "Knowing when to speak and when to hush is a delicate dance of communication that must be practiced with patience and discernment."

Think back to any experience when you ignored signs that someone should not have been trusted. Recall their actions, behaviors, key phrases, and attitudes. Let this experience be a lesson. Don't dwell on betrayal. Focus on the lesson of learning to discern.

If you pray for discernment, you will be tested, so pay close attention. Opportunities for practice will show up. What did they say? What did they avoid saying? How did they act? Make note of anything you ignored in the past, that would raise concerns for you now. This exercise will help you sharpen your discernment skills. Rational thinking, clear communication, and the ability to cut through confusion are also attributes of discernment.

Remain objective and detached. Sometimes you must focus solely on facts and logic rather than emotions. Be honest with yourself and operate in integrity as you think critically to make judgments.

NEVER IGNORE YOUR GUT

If something feels off-putting, pull back a bit and evaluate how you feel and why you feel it. If you determine that the feeling is coming from a personal bias or unhealed trauma, address the root issue within you. None of us are perfect. "Ye without sin cast the first stone."

"There are plenty of good people in the world. The question you must ask yourself daily is, 'Am I one of them?'"

When there is confusion, the best place to start is always within. Reflection, introspection, and self-awareness are key to living a peaceful triumphant life with healthy boundaries.

Operating from unhealed trauma is self-sabotage. In the past, unhealed trauma blurred my perspective and clouded my judgment, making me, my own worst enemy and my ability to properly discern, virtually nonexistent. You cannot use your past hurt as an excuse, especially when you refuse to heal it.

If you're constantly blaming others and not taking responsibility for your own actions, you will limit the advancement opportunities on your life journey. Life has levels like video games. You overcome the obstacles, slay the dragons, and rise to the next level.

New levels, new devils is true, but you'd better make sure those devils are not within you.

Sometimes the dragons are within. Each level of life gets more difficult. With each elevation, you gain greater wisdom and become stronger, and more strategic. Start where you are. Your only competition is the person in the mirror. Take responsibility and face your own shadows. Face the obstacles and learn the lessons.

Finding Peace in Solitude

Healing may call for a season of solitude because it provides the space for self-reflection, allows you to process your emotions without external pressures, and helps you reconnect with yourself.

In solitude, you can gain clarity, build inner strength, and find peace, ultimately encouraging a deeper and more thorough healing experience. Solitude should not be confused with isolation. And it's crucial not to get lost in grief or fall into hopelessness as this could lead to unhealthy isolation. A good verse to read for encouragement is 2 Corinthians 4:8-10 which reads, "We are troubled on every side, yet not distressed; we are perplexed, but not in despair; persecuted, but not forsaken; cast down, but not destroyed".

Moving in silence will give you space to heal privately and process your emotions allowing you to navigate heartbreak, sorrow, and emotional pain more effectively without judgment or pressure. It may seem like healing work will delay your progress, but taking time to heal is courageous and can save you from catastrophic mistakes on your journey. Please don't skip the healing process.

Back to the importance of discernment and listening to your gut. The worst thing I've ever done is to ignore a gut feeling that something wasn't right. It may come naturally to you to help others when you can, but remember, the stewardess' instruction, "Place the oxygen mask on yourself first."

Otherwise, you run the risk of becoming a people-pleaser and sacrificing your own mental and emotional well-being. Having a passion for supporting and uplifting others is admirable, but there must be balance and boundaries. When you connect with a person who is at a low point in life, you could become their high.

If they aren't actively doing the work to heal for themselves and continually relying on you as a source of power and strength, you risk being depleted and not having enough energy to pursue your own goals.

SOMETIMES CHASING YOUR DREAMS PLACES A TARGET ON YOUR BACK

Joseph became a target the moment he shared his dreams. His enthusiasm, confidence, and self-assurance were envied.

The level of discipline and focus necessary to plan, execute, and realize a dream is extraordinarily attractive, but sometimes attracts the unwanted attention of secret onlookers who plot, plan, and scheme.

Your resolve, however, must remain. They are distractions. Remain committed to goal setting, planning, and having the determination to see it all through. The fact that you dare to go for your dream turns you into a flame. Your courage, discipline, and determination shine in the darkness of this world. You, as a passionate flame, will attract a lot of moths.

People who have put off their dreams are tempted to target those who move forward with theirs.

They are also prone to taking shortcuts to achieve success, like stealing, killing, and destroying. People will steal ideas and claim them as their own. Content creators fall victim to this. Their content gets stolen and reposted. Or mean-spirited people report their content falsely in hopes of destroying their reputation or business. Identity theft is another example of people taking shortcuts to success at someone else's expense.

Jealous rage is also a thing among those who seek to harm others. King Saul was so jealous of David that he tried to kill him. Cain killed his brother out of jealousy because he felt rejected. Today, we hear similar news stories too often about people who lose their lives because of greed, envy, and hatred.

Protect yourself. Avoid posting your every move on social media. Try not to text too much information in the message group. Resist the urge to blurt your good news.

It takes discipline to tame your tongue and monitor your mouth, but the benefits of moving in silence will be well worth it. There will be plenty of time for celebrations and announcements once you reach your desired level!

MEMORY VERSE: PROVERBS 18:15 (NIV)

The heart of the discerning acquires knowledge, for the ears of the wise seek it out.

PRAYER

Lord, grant me a heart of discernment and a hunger for knowledge that aligns with Your truth. Help me to listen with wisdom and seek understanding in all things, so I may live a life that honors You. In Jesus' name, Amen.

AFFIRMATION

I have a discerning heart and wise ears. I seek knowledge and understanding, walking in the wisdom that God provides.

MANTRA

"With discernment, I seek knowledge; with Godly wisdom, I grow."

CHAPTER 3

THE SPIRIT OF
STEAL, KILL, & DESTROY

"Fallen" is one of the creepiest movies I've ever seen. It's an action crime thriller that delves into the supernatural. In it, Denzel Washington plays a detective who battles an unseen enemy—an ancient evil spirit capable of possessing anyone.

The thief comes only to steal and kill and destroy; I have come that they may have life, and have it to the full. -John 10:10

This movie is reminiscent of what I imagine spiritual warfare and monitoring spirits to be like. Have you ever felt like something you can't see is wreaking havoc in your life? You can't quite put your finger on it, but things just seem off. The spirit of steal, kill, and destroy (SKD) is waging a spiritual attack. Your Spirit may be picking up on a battle that you cannot physically see.

This is not the time to panic. In these seasons, seek wisdom, clarity, and guidance. Wake up every morning and put on the whole armor.

Pray throughout the day, stand steadfast, and trust in the authority God has given you to "tread on serpents, scorpions, and all manner of evil in the earth".

Know that "nothing shall by any means hurt you". Declare, "A thousand shall fall by my side, ten thousand at my right hand, but no harm shall come near my dwelling".

Monitoring spirits hover around to mess with your life's natural flow, blocking positive changes and growth. Their mission? To keep you stuck in negative cycles and prevent you from moving forward. If you stay covered in prayer, these attacks are no match for you In Jesus' name. "Do not be afraid of them; the LORD your God himself will fight for you." Deuteronomy 3:22. Watch out for the tricks—

monitoring spirits can orchestrate misunderstandings, confusion, painful endings and betrayals, leaving you feeling shattered and hopeless. If you aren't aware, you may believe that it's something you've done wrong. Or you may start to doubt your own faith. When you are close to an achievement, monitoring spirits will work overtime to influence people to help bring you down. People may start to gossip about your past, try to ruin your reputation or negatively influence the way people view you.

"People under the influence of monitoring spirits are persistent for a reason. They are on assignment."

Any personal information that you have shared with them will be used against you. All in the interest of stopping you from moving forward. Regardless of who it is, once you identify that someone is under the influence of a monitoring spirit, you need to shut it down expeditiously.

Distance yourself physically, and emotionally, and keep your business to yourself. Protect yourself. Keep the details of what's going on in your life to yourself, no matter how they try to coax it out of you. Put up a boundary and keep it up. Keeping it all balanced, try not to be paranoid and live in fear. Not everyone is out to get you. Discernment is key.

Monitoring spirits create roadblocks. They block blessings and distract you from working on your purpose.

You don't have to look for monitors, they will come to you. They will invade your space and your privacy, without welcome or warning. Some of them are quite diabolical and persistent. They will approach disguised as a devoted or concerned supporter. They show up during pivotal times in your life- both good and bad. They show up when you're experiencing hard times to feed on your pain and revel in what seems to be your defeat.

---

2 Corinthians 2: 11, **Lest Satan should get an advantage of us: for we are not ignorant of his devices.**

They show up when you are doing well to see how they can push you off your path and disrupt your progress through gossip, slander, emotional imbalance, and fear. Think about the last person who showed up and distracted you just when you were about to reach a pivotal milestone in your life. You got so wrapped up in them that you completely abandoned your dreams. Or imagine a so-called friend who dropped out of school but nags you to party when you should be studying. Or an office affair that tempts you just before a big promotion. I'm sure if you think about it you can come up with many more examples.

Sometimes it is not a physical person, but instead, an unexplained setback or chaotic event that happens at the most inconvenient time and throws you completely off balance. Think about nearly reaching a savings goal only to get blindsided by an unexpected expense or a financial setback, which forces you to dip into your savings or depletes it entirely. I am compelled to say, whether this is the result of spiritual warfare or not, start over and keep moving forward. Don't give up.

The human spirit is stronger than anything that can happen to it."

— *C.C. Scott*

Remember, monitoring spirits use anyone- family, friends, co-workers, children, clergy (yes, I said it.), the mail carrier, and the milkman for that matter. No, but seriously. I'm making light of it but, my point is that monitoring spirits will by any means necessary, use anyone they can, to steal, kill, and destroy you, your dreams, and your aspirations. A monitoring spirit will exploit anyone's vulnerability-even your own.

Everyone is tempted by his own desires as they lure him away and trap him. James 1:14 GNT

DON'T LET YOURSELF BE USED.

When we operate from a spirit of jealousy, we are susceptible to being used by monitoring spirits. Jealousy makes us vulnerable.

It will make a parent betray a child. Or a child to turn on a parent. Jealousy will turn a normally kind person into a bitter, resentful, and malicious enemy. Monitoring spirits will even influence us to self-sabotage.

Do not participate in drama. When someone informs you of what another person said, keep it in mind, but do not engage in retaliation.

Avoid gossip and speaking ill of others out of jealousy or envy. When they go low, you go high. Don't let the enemy bait you into confusion. Your focus should be balancing your life and reaching your goals. Drama, gossip, bullying, and stalking are all distraction tactics.

"Your focus is on reaching your goals. Ensnaring you in drama, chaos, and confusion is a distraction tactic of the enemy."

Monitors are dedicated to their mission. They disrespect personal boundaries and ask way too many personal questions. No matter how much you try to avoid them, they will keep looking for ways to be in your space.

People under the influence of monitoring spirits are persistent for a reason. They are on assignment. Delilah was on assignment to help the enemy destroy Sampson. Potiphar's wife was on assignment to help stop Joseph from reaching his destiny. Judas was on assignment to help the enemy destroy Jesus.

Do you know someone who seems to be on assignment to stop you or someone else? Is there something or someone that repeatedly throws you off balance?

I feel led to say here, don't be confused. The enemy's assignment will never be bigger than God's plan and purpose. So even when the enemy thinks they are winning, they're losing, because God has the final say. Only you can stop the fulfillment of your purpose.

It wasn't over until Job was restored double. It wasn't over until Joseph became a great ruler. It wasn't over until Sampson regained his strength. Consider this about Sampson, he was distracted from his God-ordained purpose because he shared too much information with a persistent monitoring spirit, Delilah.

God turned Sampson's mess into this message, you cannot tell everybody your business. Some things are meant to remain between you and God. Another important point we learn from Sampson is not to entertain people, places, or things that appeal to our weaknesses and tempt us away from God's plan for us.

Protect yourself through prayer; set boundaries, and foster a nurturing, stable environment. Admit your vices and actively do the healing work. Focus on creating a secure and abundant home life. "A family that prays together stays together". Take care of your well-being. Ill health- whether emotional or physical will make you vulnerable to attacks because of your weakened state. Take care of your temple. It is the fortress of your soul.

Be sober-minded, alert, and discerning. It is vital to maintain mental clarity. 1 Peter 4:7 says, "The end of all things is near. Therefore, be alert and of sober mind so that you may pray."

Establish firm boundaries with people and communicate assertively to keep monitoring spirits in their place- and by *place*, I mean far-far away from you! Cut through deception and confusion with logic and truth. Be clear about what you mean and mean it when you say it.

The devil has nothing to do with the truth. There is no truth in him. It is expected of the devil to lie, for he is a liar and the father of lies. *John 8:44*

Building your confidence will also protect you. Stay hopeful, and positive, and pray without ceasing. Having a spirit of a sound mind, power, and love can repel negativity. Stay hopeful. Hype yourself up periodically. This keeps your confidence high and makes you less likely to be brought down by tactics of a monitoring spirit. If you feel rejected in any way- from a person, a job, or an opportunity, don't let it create insecurity. And as you achieve small goals, celebrate yourself. This will improve your mood and make you feel better overall. See the situation for what it is and adopt a positive perspective. A positive perspective lowers your chances of being overcome by feelings of fear and doubt. It also helps to draw strength from positive victories of your past. You succeeded before and you can do it again!

Important Takeaways

Confidence and inner strength are crucial. Being assertive and maintaining a strong, positive presence can deter negativity. Don't be tricked by anyone posing as kind, caring, and friendly. You don't have to be cold and unsocial. You may miss out on a beautiful opportunity. Just be discerning. Sometimes being discerning can look like you slowing down and not impulsively jumping into commitments. Harmonious relationships are important but discern who you are aligning yourself with.

Aligning yourself with people who operate from a spirit of love and harmony can provide protection. "Where two or three are gathered together, there will God be in the midst".

Monitoring spirits are no match for strong, loving connections grounded in faith, love, and emotional maturity. Later we will talk more about what to look for in an ideal team of Purpose Partners or your *Purpose Team*.

Do not give your power to others but know that strategic alliances are powerful. Just seek guidance from God before you seek it from anyone else. The advice you receive from others should be confirmation of what the Holy Spirit has already told you. Be aware of your power to lead and create your reality. Your ability to confidently lead your own life helps protect you from being redirected by monitors who aim to throw you off course. Use prayer and discernment to protect yourself. Harnessing your inner power and focusing it with intention will keep you on track protected from distractions. "Lay aside every weight and sin that so easily throws you off course". Hebrews 12:1. Trust the guidance of the Holy Spirit and be compassionate towards yourself. "My sheep know my voice. The voice of a stranger they will not follow." John 10:27.

Victory Over Monitoring Spirits

Building a strong support network is essential in providing spiritual and emotional resilience against the influence of monitoring spirits. Surround yourself with those who share your values and are aligned with your goals. By seeking the support and prayers of like-minded individuals, you create a united front that is more difficult for the enemy to penetrate. Again, "A family that prays together stays together"—this principle extends beyond family and holds true for any network of believers. A united group of prayer warriors is a powerful defense, standing together in faith against any opposition.

Comfort During Attacks

The Comforter (Holy Spirit) helps us with the debilitating effects of anxiety and fear that monitoring spirits might try to induce. By providing comfort and reassurance, The Comforter aids in alleviating our worries and fears. The Holy Spirit reminds us that much of what we fear is a tactic of the enemy to attack our minds. The Comforter encourages us to remember our power, pray for peace, and seek wisdom. Commit to standing firm when you have setbacks and disruptions. Try not to allow them to permanently knock you off balance or lose your focus. Remember that monitoring spirits want to find out information about you so they can use it against you and somehow cause destruction, but they can't use what they don't know. Move in silence. Work-life balance and proper self-care are important defenses to spiritual attacks. By managing our responsibilities and staying flexible, we can better handle challenges. Exhaustion opens the door to confusion, illness, and errors. Work-life balance is key to staying on track and making forward progress. Proverbs 12:1 (NIV) says, *"Whoever loves discipline loves knowledge, but whoever hates correction is stupid."*

Ouch!

You may be tempted to feel defeated by the havoc that a monitoring spirit has already caused in your life. But remember, you are not alone in this battle and you have spiritual guards. "For he will command his angels concerning you to guard you in all your ways; they will lift you up in their hands so that you will not strike your foot against a stone."- Psalm 91:11-12. We are empowered by hope, faith, and a strong sense of purpose; *"God hasn't given us a spirit of fear but of sound mind, power, and love."* We must learn to lead our own lives and take authority. This strong, positive faith mindset acts as a shield against negative influences. Spiritual maturity teaches us resilience and perseverance, helping us to establish and maintain boundaries and our unwavering faith and steadfastness create a protective hedge. Pray without ceasing and put on your spiritual armor daily. Ephesians 6:10-18 warns, "Finally, my brethren, be strong in the Lord, and in the power of his might. Put on the whole armor of God, that ye may be able to stand against the wiles of the devil…" If you need a reason to move in silence, let the message in this chapter be it. Monitoring spirits are another strong reminder of why discretion is essential. Like in the movie, spirits of steal, kill, and destroy can operate through living beings – human or animal. I'm reminded of the story in Matthew 8 about Jesus casting the demons into the pigs.

---

1 So the devils besought him, saying, If thou cast us out, suffer us to go away into the herd of swine. 32 And he said unto them, Go. And when they were come out, they went into the herd of swine: and, behold, the whole herd of swine ran violently down a steep place into the sea, and perished in the waters. -Matthew 8:31-32

Monitoring spirits will work through people to throw distractions and false paths your way, they try to steer you off course from your true goals and purpose. Think of the person who wiggles their way into your life, gets to know everything about you, and then proceeds to betray you in the worst possible way. As a result, you become depressed, broken, and discouraged. You shut down and stop caring for yourself, let alone pursuing your goals.

DISCERNING A SPIRIT OF SKD

Sometimes you can recognize a person under the influence of a monitoring spirit by their subtle body language, the things they say, or the tone in which they speak. Be mindful that people don't always know that they are under this influence. Furthermore, none of us are exempt as targets. That's one reason you should avoid gossip. Your words could be used to hurt someone else, whether you intend or not. Sometimes it's obvious when someone is under the steal, kill, destroy influence.

These people are outright evil. They walk away when you are talking or interrupt your good news because they don't want to hear it. They may gather a group to gang up on you and make evil intentions known publicly. Their goal is to ignore you and your accomplishments and to make you feel alone.

When a monitoring spirit is a bit more subtle, you will have to pay closer attention. Like they say, eyes are the window to the soul. You can identify a person under the influence of a monitoring spirit by their eyes. Pay attention to the subtle changes in eye movements and expressions when you talk. These things happen in an instant, so you may miss them at first, but as your discernment grows, you will be able to notice them more clearly. I have personally witnessed (and ignored), during communication, these non-verbal warning signs of a steal, kill, and destroy spirited individual:

- Rolling eyes in disgust
- Glaring with envy
- Blank stares as if you are boring them
- Snarling or growling sounds
- Heavily sighing to show disinterest

Keeping it all balanced, not everyone who exhibits these signs is under the influence of a monitoring spirit. Some people are just expressive. They may also be going through something at the time of your discussion. This is why prayer and discernment are key.If you want to succeed, you need energy, emotional well-being, and clarity to keep moving forward with momentum. Monitoring spirits aim to weaken your emotional resilience and block your healing process. So if they can use others to redirect your focus to painful memories, irritate your soul, and drain your motivation, then they can and will stall your progress or keep you from moving forward altogether. When you observe these behaviors, don't cause a scene or feel like you need to "call it out". Make a mental note and in your time of solitude, pray and ask for guidance, but don't ignore it.

---

1 Peter 5:8, Be sober, be vigilant, because your adversary the devil walketh about as a roaring lion, seeking whom he may devour.

Let's wrap up this chapter about monitoring spirits on an inspirational note. Here are several ways The Comforter supports us as we move in silence and face weapons formed by monitoring spirits. The Holy Spirit empowers us by:

- Helping us manage and reduce our fears and anxieties, providing comfort and clarity.
- Aiding us in remaining balanced and adaptable, effectively managing our priorities, and staying grounded.
- Instilling confidence, vision, and leadership qualities in us, helping us take charge and lead with strength.
- Teaching us resilience and perseverance, ensuring that we establish and maintain protective boundaries.

- Giving us the inner strength and courage needed to face challenges and overcome negative influences with compassion and patience.
- Lastly, the Holy Spirit helps us by orchestrating collaborations. Angels in human form will cross our path to help us alleviate fear, maintain balance, encourage resilience, and open doors of opportunities.

You can still succeed and progress despite attempts to steal, kill, and destroy your plans. Don't be discouraged if you've been outwitted by monitoring spirits in the past. We live and we learn, especially through setbacks, obstacles, and mistakes. These lessons help us grow and evolve.

Colossians 1:13 says, "For he has rescued us from the dominion of darkness and brought us into the kingdom of the Son he loves."

MEMORY VERSE: 1 JOHN 3:8

He that committeth sin is of the devil; for the devil sinneth from the beginning. For this purpose, the Son of God was manifested, that he might destroy the works of the devil.

PRAYER

Lord Jesus, thank You for coming to destroy the works of the devil in my life and for granting me victory over sin and darkness. Protect me from every scheme of the enemy and let Your light shine through my life. I stand secure in Your power and grace. In Jesus' name, Amen.

AFFIRMATION

Through Jesus Christ, the works of the devil are destroyed in my life. I am shielded by God's power. I walk in freedom and victory every day.

MANTRA

Jesus has won; I walk in His victory and protection.

CHAPTER 4

THEIR PROJECTION IS NOT YOUR REALITY

I'm reminded of the term, object of affection. When you are the object of someone's affection, that means they have a great deal of emotion for you. They think fondly of you. There is a special place in their heart just for you.

The object of your affection could be a special gift, a pet, or anything with which you feel a deep connection. You pour emotion onto that object for as long as you feel strongly about it. Such affections can last a lifetime or leave as soon as our attention is turned toward a different object. Now let's talk about projection. Projection occurs when someone attributes their thoughts, feelings, or motives to another. Again, in this circumstance, you are the object of another's attention. However, it is not just affection being poured onto you. I like to explain it like this. Imagine a person you encounter as a walking movie projector. Something about you draws them in. Now you are their big screen of choice.

You are the screen onto which they will project the movie of their beliefs. The movie could be a romcom, action, or horror. It depends on their belief system. Whatever they think, feel, or believe, they project it onto you so that you appear to others as *they* believe you ought.

Instead of taking accountability and healing their belief system, a negative projector accuses you, the object of their projection. Though the projector has the issue, it appears to everyone else as if you do because you, the big screen, are the one on display. Projection allows people to escape their demons and scapegoat you instead.

They tell people that you are jealous of them and then they project onto you so that it looks like it is true. Projectors are the people that your elders warned you about. The people who throw rocks and hide their hands. Projecting is a way for people to deal with feelings or behaviors they feel may be unacceptable by seeing them in others instead of themselves.

For example, someone who is angry at their boss might accuse another coworker of being disgruntled and unhappy. A person who feels inadequate might accuse others of being overly critical of them.

WHY DO PEOPLE PROJECT NEGATIVITY?

People who project often avoid dealing with their hidden fears and insecurities. They might be confused or unable to see things clearly, leading them to project their internal struggles onto those around them.

Due to past traumas, social pressure, or a lack of clarity, they may find themselves struggling to communicate their true feelings. This drives them to use negativity as a defense mechanism to mask their vulnerability.

This could be due to a fixed mindset or a negative belief system. A fixed mindset is when someone believes their abilities, intelligence, or talents are set in stone and can't change

People with this mindset give up easily when things get tough. To them working hard is pointless if there are no immediate results. Thinking like this will hold you back because it stops you from learning and growing over time. They feel a lack, therefore they project it. They lack motivation, inspiration, and drive. This way of thinking is a hamster wheel. If they stay on it, they will remain stuck in their ways breeding more hostility and lack of accountability.

Let's be real. We all are susceptible to this or have been. If this describes you currently and you find yourself projecting your insecurities and inner turmoil onto others, you *can* transform. It starts by renewing your mind.

This transformation will help you embrace a more beneficial growth mindset, establish healthier coping mechanisms, heal lack mindset, and develop your emotional intelligence. You can pull yourself out of this pit.

7 THINGS TO UNDERSTAND ABOUT PEOPLE WHO PROJECT

1. **They have hidden fears and insecurities**. They are often dealing with their hidden fears and illusions, causing them to project negativity.

2. **They cannot cope with feelings of inadequacy**. They might feel inadequate or threatened by others' success, leading to negative projection.

3. **They tend to react impulsively**. They may project negativity impulsively in response to rapid changes or difficult communication.

4. **They have distorted perceptions**. Their projections stem from a distorted view of reality and their internal fantasies or fears.

5. **They may lack clarity**: They struggle with clear thinking and emotional honesty, using negativity as a defense mechanism.

6. **They need a shift in their perspective**. They are stuck in negative patterns and need to see things from a new, more positive point of view.

7. **They're experiencing inner turmoil and conflict**. Their negativity often reflects their inner conflicts and feelings of defeat.

By recognizing these aspects of projection, you can better understand the root causes in others and respond by quietly and strategically distancing yourself.

Know when someone is projecting. It is entirely possible to absorb projected emotions and confuse them with yours. You may have experienced this without realizing it. Think of a time when another person entered the room and the mood of everyone else in the room changed. Or someone called you to vent about their relationship and for the remainder of the day you were angry with your partner.

Chances are, you sponged up their energy. A dead giveaway is when you feel uneasy or sad without cause and you have no clue as to why. Upon reflection, you realize this feeling came on immediately after speaking to or thinking about a particular person, situation, or circumstance. Before you sink into a dark emotional abyss, stop and think, "Is this really how I feel, or is it how they feel?"

"You don't have to subscribe to other people's issues" -unknown

---

If your imbalanced emotions are the issue, seek guidance and implement changes, but if you are generally in a good mood until you encounter *them*, consider distancing yourself. Evaluate the connection.

Another thing to look out for is people who attempt to impose fears, insecurities, or negative behaviors onto you. They tell you to fear seeking better because they are afraid to seek better. Or the opposite, they convince you that something is bad for you because their circumstance is bad for them. Be careful of projectors, because they will go as far as to spread false information about you to others.

Another sign of someone projecting negativity is when conflicts arise, their goal is winning the argument, not resolving the issue. They project emotionally or using words. If they can make you look like the unstable one, they have won, and you are left feeling confused and emotionally drained. Years ago, I heard a speaker say, that when we allow others to get us out of character, we give them our power.

I believe we do more than that. We open ourselves up to the spirits of steal, kill, and destroy. And also, we give credit to the projector's false claims. "The devil is the accuser of the brethren". Make no mistake, anyone who is projecting negative BS is operating from the spirit of SKD. They want to assert control or dominance over you. By coming across as overly authoritative, they hope to instill fear and self-doubt. Some will even try the tactic of ignoring your wishes and imposing their own. This is meant to make you feel unworthy and unimportant.

Projection could look like an overly critical boss, constantly questioning your actions or motives, and frequently engaging in arguments with you. Try as you might, your performance is never good enough in their eyes. They may even ignore your areas of accomplishment or take credit for themselves while claiming you are not qualified to be promoted. Their behavior can be a sign that they are projecting their insecurities onto you.

Another tool of projection is deceit. The Negative BS projector will use lies and manipulation to control outcomes so that they can spread misinformation and go undetected.

How can you deal with people who project their negativity onto you?

The battle is first fought in your mind. First, remember that these individuals are unhealed. Something happened to them in the past that deeply affected their belief system, and this negative projection is how they cope with that. While it is not your responsibility to heal them, it is your responsibility to model healthy behavior. Healthy behavior does not involve causing a scene or doing something that invites negative consequences. "Listen carefully: I am sending you out like sheep among wolves; so be wise as serpents, and innocent as doves."

Second, have a good understanding of who you are. Know who you are in your soul, without doubt, so that when someone tries to project onto you, they cannot succeed because you are wise enough to discern the movie they are projecting represents their story, not yours.

"Wisdom is the principal thing; therefore, get wisdom: and with all thy getting get understanding."

Thirdly, communicate clearly. When someone attempts to project their burdens onto you, that is the time to communicate your position clearly and not confrontationally- so that there is no doubt about your position or beliefs- if you care to do so.

There is no need for aggression, violence, or profanity. Simply, state your position, respectfully. This will help clear up any confusion for those witnessing the projection. In some instances, this will put an end to the confusion immediately. It may also discourage the projector from future attempts. "The words of the reckless pierce like swords, but the tongue of the wise brings healing."

Handle the situations with maturity. You can also try distancing yourself as much as possible. Don't put yourself in situations where you are being used as a screen. If the negative projector hangs out in the breakroom, avoid them in the breakroom setting.

Avoidance, however, is not always the best way to deal with a projector. They may take your kindness for weakness and at some point, you may have to address them.

"If your brother or sister offends you, go and point out their fault, just between the two of you. If they listen to you, you have won them over." Matthew 18:15

Prayer and discernment are needed. The Holy Spirit may lead you to pick your battles. In this case, you may be guided away from the situation for a healthier, more fulfilling environment.

"Evil company corrupts good habits." Distancing yourself from the negative projectors is important for several reasons. First, it helps protect your self-esteem. When you avoid negativity, you prevent damage to your self-confidence and self-worth, which can lead to self-doubt.

Second, it keeps your emotional health in check by shielding you from the stress, anxiety, and depression that come from constant negativity. Additionally, it helps you maintain a positive mindset, allowing you to stay motivated and focused on your goals without being dragged down by negative influence. Constant negative projection can suck the life out of you. At first, you don't notice it. Slowly you begin to feel less like yourself. Over time, you lose motivation and begin to doubt your previous dreams are relevant, let alone possible. You will feel the opposite in a positive environment because it will boost your productivity and creativity, making it easier for you to achieve your goals effectively. Finally, distancing yourself from a negative projector establishes a healthy boundary. It shows that you value your mental and emotional well-being, creating a positive mental and emotional space where you can thrive and grow.

9 SIGNS THEY MAY BE PROJECTING THEIR NEGATIVITY ONTO YOU

1. They impose their fears or insecurities onto you.
2. They convince others that their toxic behavior is your fault.
3. They leave you feeling sad or defeated.
4. Their actions or words frequently lead to confusion.
5. They try to assert control or dominance over you.
6. They are overly critical or confrontational.
7. They act deceitfully or dishonestly, making you question their intentions.
8. They display jealousy and attempt to undermine your successes and achievements.
9. Their negativity makes you want to distance yourself.

Oversharing can make you a target for negative projection and expose you to harsh criticism and judgment, making it harder to maintain objective and strategic thinking. Success shared too early or in the wrong environment can attract envy or scrutiny. The solution: stop telling everybody your plans, goals, and personal details. Move in silence. By recognizing these risks, you can better understand the importance of discretion and the potential negative consequences of oversharing.

Topic	Scripture
Your Finances Are Blessed	*Deuteronomy 28:12* – "The Lord will open the heavens... to bless all the work of your hands."
Your Career Is Blessed	*Proverbs 16:3* – "Commit your work to the Lord, and your plans will be established."
Your Health Is Blessed	*Jeremiah 30:17* – "For I will restore health to you, and your wounds I will heal, declares the Lord."
Your Children Are Blessed	*Isaiah 54:13* – "All your children shall be taught by the Lord, and great shall be the peace of your children."
Your Home Is Blessed	*Proverbs 3:33* – "The Lord's curse is on the house of the wicked, but he blesses the home of the righteous."
Your Relationship Is Blessed	*Ecclesiastes 4:9-10* – "Two are better than one... if either of them falls down, one can help the other up."
Your Business Is Blessed	*Psalm 90:17* – "May the favor of the Lord our God rest on us; establish the work of our hands for us."
Your Bloodline Is Blessed	*Genesis 12:3* – "And I will bless those who bless you... and in you all the families of the earth shall be blessed."

MEMORY VERSE: REVELATION 12:10 (AMPLIFIED)

Then I heard a voice from heaven shout, "Our God has shown his saving power, and his kingdom has come! God's own Chosen One has shown his authority. Satan accused our people in the presence of God day and night. Now he has been thrown out!

PRAYER

Heavenly Father, thank You for Your salvation, power, and authority in my life. I praise You for the victory over the accuser who seeks to condemn me. Through Christ, I am free from every charge brought against me. Strengthen my faith, Oh Lord, and remind me daily that Your kingdom reigns supreme. Let Your power and authority guide my steps. Father, I ask that every voice seeking to discourage me is silenced. In Jesus' name, Amen.

AFFIRMATION: I am redeemed. God's power and salvation reign in my life. The accuser's charges against me hold no weight because I am covered by the blood of Jesus and I walk in His authority.

MANTRA: God's kingdom reigns, Christ's authority prevails, and I stand victorious.

CHAPTER 5

STOP TELLING PEOPLE ABOUT YOUR RELATIONSHIPS

The best team members for achieving your dreams are those who are equally yoked with you. I call them *Purpose Partners*. We must build relationships with people who share our values, beliefs, and goals so that we grow together.

These Purpose Team members are invaluable. You will keep each other grounded and motivated, especially when things get tough. Equally yoked friendships feel naturally balanced and make your journey through life a lot more fulfilling.

Be ye not unequally yoked together with unbelievers: for what fellowship hath righteousness with unrighteousness? and what communion hath light with darkness? 2 Corinthians 6:14-18

Pray that equally yoked relationships be placed on your path. As you pursue your dreams, you will be challenged on all sides spiritually, mentally, and emotionally. Equally yoked friends offer empathy, understanding, and solutions. Never underestimate the power of an equally yoked ally.

"If you want to go fast, go alone. If you want to go far, go together." -Proverb

---

A capable network will bring experience to the table. They may have skills and resources that complement yours, but not necessarily the same. They bring integrity to the table as they are honest and will keep you honest in your dealings and decisions. Have you ever felt overwhelmed and completely confused, but shortly after speaking with an equally yoked individual, you felt clearer, more at peace, and uplifted? These are the people you want around you most.

These are spouses, best friends, family members, business associates, and acquaintances. These people are on a whole other level and sent by God to support you. They harmonize with you beyond human DNA.

You will identify them by their strong work ethic, loyal hearts, and compassionate nature. Their support helps you maintain a hopeful and visionary perspective that will be invaluable on your journey to the promised land.

They have your back and provide honest feedback and insightful advice. They help you maintain clarity and focus on your goals. They won't enable negative beliefs and will come through with loving support when others will not.

A supportive network lays a solid foundation for future success. It gives you an advantage when starting your next endeavor because you'll be ahead with an experienced team in place. It's like building highways instead of traveling dirt roads—you'll move faster and reach your destination more smoothly.

Iron sharpens iron. *Proverbs 27:17*

A dream support team helps you grow and evolve. Surrounding yourself with successful leaders encourages you to step up in your own life. Their support stokes your leadership fires so you can achieve your passions.

To recap, this group supports you with:

- Creating a stable foundation
- Achieving fulfillment
- Bringing joy and success
- Providing clarity and insight
- Fostering collaboration and friendship
- Building long-term success
- Cultivating abundance and leadership

MAKING BODY, SOUL, & SPIRIT CONNECTIONS

The soul is comprised of your mind, will, imagination, and emotions. Purpose Partners stimulate your mind with intelligent communication; inspire you to care for your health and encourage you to feed your spirit with the word of God. These are people who encourage growth in all areas of your life. If this person is already in your life, you are blessed. Call them and say, "I appreciate you."

Now there are diversities of gifts, but the same Spirit. and there are differences of administrations, but the same Lord. And there are diversities of operations, but it is the same God which worketh all in all. But the manifestation of the Spirit is given to every man to profit withal. 1 Corinthians 12:4-7

When surrounding yourself with supporters, select people who walk in wisdom, have strong discernment; and walk by faith. "You will know a tree by the fruit it bears." You must use discernment when connecting with others. This process shouldn't be rushed. Observe people over time. This is not the same as passing judgment on someone because they aren't where you think they ought to be. Pray and ask for clarity. Don't take for granted that everyone with a title is operating in love.

Wisdom Seekers. People who seek wisdom from the Holy Spirit, knowledge, and understanding. They make a great support network. These people have gained valuable wisdom through experience. They are open to imparting knowledge to you, the student when you're ready. This guidance helps you apply their knowledge to your journey, avoid common pitfalls, and achieve your goals with clarity and purpose. While it may seem counterintuitive, having people who can challenge your perspective and help you rebuild after a crisis is beneficial. These individuals provide wisdom that brings transformation in difficult times.

Discerners of Spirits: This group has keen discernment. They see clearly what is right and what is wrong. They know the difference between truth and falsehood. People blessed with powerful discernment help you find equilibrium when you feel unstable and guide you in regaining your balance. Having them in your corner gives you spiritual insight and adds protection from deception. They are good at managing multiple responsibilities because they can see all aspects. They help you discern people, problems, and opportunities so that you make confident decisions.

Faith Warriors. You'll want to connect with supporters who "walk by faith and not by sight". There will be times on your journey when you will have to take risks. You need people with you who will stand in faith for a victorious outcome. Too, you need people of faith who can help you believe when you are tempted to doubt. They will stand by your side during tough times, offering support and solidarity. These people understand hardship and can provide empathy and practical help when needed.

Healers: Some have the gift of healing. They heal through words, prayer, and physical touch. On your journey, you will be attacked. It will be a blessing to have healers around you who will bring comfort, restoration, and peace to your spirit, soul, and body. Healers want to see you well and they want to see you succeed. They promote well-being.

10 GREEN FLAGS OF A PURPOSE PARTNER

1. **Compassionate and Kind-Hearted**: They provide emotional support and comfort yet keep you honest.
2. **Supportive During Hard Times**: They have your back and offer empathy and practical help.
3. **Emotionally Intelligent and Nurturing**: Provide understanding and compassion.
4. **Open-Minded and Encouraging**: Encourage healthy risk-taking and new opportunities.
5. **Challenging and Transformative**: Offer strength and insight during times of chaos.
6. **Balanced and Harmonious**: Promote balance, peace, and patience in your life.
7. **Stable and Dependable**: Provide guidance, structure, and practical advice.
8. **Enthusiastic and Creative**: Inspire and motivate with new ideas and energy.
9. **Adaptable and Practical**: Help you manage and maneuver through change.
10. **Passionate and Action-Oriented**: Encourage the pursuit of your ambitions with drive and motivation.

By surrounding yourself with individuals who possess these qualities, you can build a strong and supportive network that helps you navigate life's challenges and achieve your goals. Seek people who complement your morals and beliefs. You don't have to search for people who are carbon copies of yourself. Our differences make us unique and having differing perspectives is always a positive in any real network circle.   It goes without saying that your relationship with Purpose Partners should evolve as you grow and develop personally and professionally. Personalities change and the network you have today, may not be the network you harmonize with in the future. People who have "Purpose Partner" characteristics understand this and are mature enough to recognize when the relationship is no longer symbiotic. God forbid, but you may discover down the line, that you have a Judas in your circle. Whatever the case, when parties are no longer meshing, it's time to move on – without malice, ill will, or hard feelings. Forgive and take the steps necessary to move on.

12 RED FLAGS OF PURPOSE BLOCKERS

1. **Doubtful**: Lack confidence in their own abilities, which prevents them from taking advantage of opportunities.
2. **Jealous and envious**: Feel resentful of others' successes and may undermine them.
3. **Fearful of change**: Prefer to stay in their comfort zone and resist new opportunities.
4. **Chronic complainer**: Frequently voices dissatisfaction without seeking solutions.
5. **Procrastinator**: Delay taking action leading to missed opportunities.
6. **Overly critical**: Harshly judgmental of others.
7. **Victim mentality**: View themselves as perpetual victims.
8. **Self-Centered**: Focus primarily on their own needs and without considering others.
9. **Stubborn**: Refuse to change their mind or approach even when it's necessary.
10. **Unforgiving**: Hold grudges and never forgive past mistakes.
11. **Jealous**: Feel insecure and threatened by others' achievements.
12. **Ungrateful**: Don't appreciate what they have or acknowledge the help they receive.

KEEPING IT ALL BALANCED.

If you recognize some aspect of your personality in the list of red flags; good for you! We've all experienced some of these traits at some point or another. Congratulations on being self-aware. None of us are perfect and we all have areas for growth and development. We are not here to throw stones.

Any one of us can live in a glass house and that house can be shattered if it's hit by the "right" rock. Around here, we use stones to build, not break.

Commit today, to do better for you. It's never too late to start and since you are moving in silence, no one else needs to know. Whatever the issue, find some literature, watch some videos; join anonymous groups. Find what works for you and invest in yourself.

If the issue is within you, address it and set boundaries. If the issue is with someone else, address it and set boundaries.

Reflection and self-awareness are powerful tools for personal growth and expansion, that allow us to gain insights into our own thoughts, behaviors, and experiences. This is how we make meaningful changes in our lives. It's an inside job. Not only will you become a more evolved person, but you will also show up more positively for your circle and beyond, perhaps becoming a Purpose Partner in someone else's network.

KEEP YOUR NETWORK MEMBERS UNDER WRAPS

Move in silence regarding the members of your network. Some of these people live under the radar for their own reasons. The last thing you want to do is interrupt their peace. If people know that they are supporting you, they may try to befriend your connections for nefarious reasons. Interferences and distractions can arise from others knowing details about your support team. Also, if the members of your network prefer to remain anonymous, you should respect their wishes. Your discretion and confidentiality put you in a good light. It also preserves the respect and trust of other Purpose Partners. Keeping your relationship details to yourself helps you avoid potential conflicts or jealousy from others knowing too much about your relationships. Without external distractions, you will be free to develop genuine, solid relationships.

MAINTAIN BALANCE IN THE RELATIONSHIP

When we have healthy relationship dynamics, we benefit from equal reciprocity.

Don't settle for being used and misused, with the assumption that God is going to eventually balance the situation out for you. Sometimes He is waiting for you to remove yourself.

God warns, "Touch not my anointed ones," but we must learn to set boundaries. Our lack of boundaries can allow others to gain access that God never intended for them to have. "You reap what you sow." If you're always sowing, but never reaping, something is out of balance, and you have the spiritual authority to equalize it. There should be a balance in giving and receiving time, information, and support, not just in our support network, but in our workplace, family, and daily interactions. Remember I mentioned discernment and common sense? We shouldn't go around expecting reciprocity in every single circumstance. For example, when we help someone in need, we shouldn't stand around with outstretched hands waiting for them to reciprocate. We don't perform nice deeds to receive rewards. Offering wisdom, prayers, and compassion are acts of service. Likewise, we should not act from a place of entitlement. Just because some have succeeded doesn't mean they are obligated to give their time, energy, or expertise without discernment. In short, don't allow yourself to be used, and don't use others. When you give from your heart, your heart will reward you with joy.

11 CHARACTERISTICS OF THE "EQUALLY YOKED"

1. **Creative**: They bring new ideas and perspectives to the table.
2. **Empathetic**: They understand and share the feelings of others.
3. **Dependable**: They follow through on commitments and promises.
4. **Honest & Loyal**: They stand for what is right. They have your back through good times and bad.
5. **Good Communicators**: They express ideas clearly and listen actively.
6. **Respectful and Accountable**: They value others' opinions and boundaries & take responsibility for their actions.
7. **Open-Minded**: They are willing to consider different viewpoints.
8. **Inspiring**: They motivate you to achieve your best.

9. **Resourceful**: They find solutions and offer helpful resources.
10. **Patient and Flexible**: They understand that progress takes time and effort.
11. **Passionate**: They are enthusiastic and committed to shared goals.

In closing, assembling an equally yoked team of Purpose Partners is essential as you pursue your dreams and aspirations. With equally yoked believers by your side, your chances of success are greatly enhanced. These individuals are invaluable key players in your journey. Seek out those who are equally yoked and who complement your energy. Remember to reciprocate their support as well.

There is no need to aggressively hunt these people and beg for their support. Pray for the right connections, place yourself in positive environments, and allow God to orchestrate the introduction. Pray before you make any sudden moves.

If you already have loyal, supportive, people in your life, who respect your boundaries and give you wise counsel when you need it, do not take them for granted. Recognize their value and express your gratitude by reciprocating with love and respect. Certain Purpose Partners may be temporary. As the saying goes, "People enter our life for a reason, season, or a lifetime". The people in your network may have a specific assignment, to help you through a tough time, which is their reason for your connection. Once they have helped you through that season of your life, they may move on from you and that is okay. Trust the process.

MEMORY VERSE: PROVERBS 11:14 (AMPLIFIED)

Where there is no [wise, intelligent] guidance, the people fall [and go off course like a ship without a helm], But in the abundance of [wise and godly] counselors there is victory.

PRAYER

Lord, I thank You for the gift of wise and godly counsel. Guide me as I seek advice from those who walk in your light with truth and wisdom. Help me remain humble and receptive to their guidance. Holy Spirit, lead me on the path set before me. May I never stray but walk in victory through the counsel You provide. In Jesus' name, Amen.

AFFIRMATION

I surround myself with wise and godly counselors who guide me in truth, and through their wisdom, I achieve victory in all I do.

MANTRA

Wisdom guides me, godly counsel strengthens me, and victory is mine.

CHAPTER 6

STOP TELLING PEOPLE ABOUT YOUR FAILURES

Some people will pay for a front-row seat to watch you struggle. People operating from an SKD spirit love it when you talk about your failures. They salivate over your financial problems and relationship drama.

They secretly enjoy watching you work hard on your dream only to experience a setback. But understand this, no matter how many setbacks you encounter, God will orchestrate a solution. He is a God of divine order. Make peace with the fact that every solution won't be miraculous. What I say next may not sit well so hear me out. Don't just hear this next statement with your ears. Hear it with your soul.

99.99 percent of the time, God does not consider your problem an emergency.

Hopefully, with discernment and careful planning, you can avoid the need for an emergency intervention from God. God moves in His timing. He loves you unconditionally but has already established a complex system, by which faith moves mountains.

Through my setbacks, I have come to respect God's order more than ever. Whether the setback is an attack from SKD or a consequence of my decisions, I respect God's timing, wisdom, and the lessons each experience imparts.

Joseph's story teaches us how to trust God, even when we don't understand our circumstances. Being thrown into prison because of Potiphar's wife's lie must have seemed like the worst possible setback.

Yet, Joseph remained faithful, and God stayed with him. Even in the midst of his challenges, God granted Joseph favor. "Potiphar was furious when he heard his wife's story about how Joseph had treated her. So he took Joseph and threw him into the prison where the king's prisoners were held, and there he remained. But the Lord was with Joseph in the prison and showed him his faithful love. And the Lord made Joseph a favorite with the prison warden." Genesis 39:19-21. It's important to stay in constant communication with God. "Call unto me, and I will answer thee, and show thee great and mighty things, which thou knowest not." Jeremiah 33:3. Trust God for favor in every situation. Again, God is a God of mighty works and miracles. If we need miracles, as His children, we can ask.

But, we must also be spiritually mature enough to recognize our behavior patterns to ensure we are not putting ourselves in repeated patterns of needing an emergency.

That said, there will be times when patience is required, in fact, 99.99 percent of the time. People, places, or things need to be moved around or out of the way. Events and meetings need to be orchestrated. God can and has performed miracles. Your breakthrough can happen in the blink of an eye and if that's what you need ask for it. But this section is about patience.

You must respect the heavenly algorithm and give it time to work in your favor.

Your faith will be tested as you move forward. This is how we learn and grow. "We go from faith to faith and glory to glory". A setback can be temporary or permanent, depending on how you respond to it. It's not a dead end, but rather a crossroad of opportunity.

Pause, pray, reevaluate, and move forward with greater clarity. "Let us run with perseverance the race God has for us." If God puts you in the race, you'd better believe He will give you the tools to finish it. You bring the perseverance and the patience; God will bring the provision and favor. Hopefully, you have a safe network of Purpose Partners around you, but if not, seek answers and solutions privately through online sources, networks, and learning materials. Keep your options open and reflect without displaying distress around the wrong people.

Now there are always exceptions to the rule (not that I'm creating any rules). Some people experience setbacks, post their situation on social media, and receive a tremendous outpouring of love and support from the community.

I think these beautiful stories are the exceptions. It doesn't work for everyone. So again, pray and use your discernment. Some people mean well, and you may get a lot of well-wishes, but you must be careful airing out your business. Once you open that door, it is difficult to close, and people you don't know start to weigh in on your business and worse feel entitled to your time and energy.

When Job experienced his extreme setback, He was devastated. In his case, he couldn't help but have an audience. He lost everything and his friends judged him. Their questions and accusations made him feel worse. So much so that Job began to wonder if God was punishing him. When you experience a setback, your doubts and fears are overwhelming enough without the added pressure of others' probing and judgments, which only make things worse and slow your progress. It's like trying to put out a fire while the wrong people around you are spewing gasoline on it.

It's good to have people around that you can trust, but sometimes all you need is peace, solitude, and faith to come up with the right solution to your problem.

Discreetly handling disappointments involves processing the loss, redirecting your focus to finding a solution, and looking for opportunities for growth and renewal.

Keeping it all balanced, God can and will, true to His nature, turn your perceived setback into a testimony. "He will prepare a table before you in the presence of your enemy". Trying not to fall apart at the seams is easier said than done. In some cases, releasing the pain through tears is the most healing thing you can do. I've yelled into a pillow a few times in the past. Afterward, I cried a good cry and allowed myself to feel my feelings. Sometimes you sleep better after a good cry. Our feelings are valid, but just because we feel something doesn't mean it's true. Just because you feel hopeless doesn't mean you're done for.

Agony must have been what Job felt as his world crashed around him, but he didn't question God publicly. Even when his wife told him to curse God and die. You see the people around you when they see you down, they want you to admit defeat and yield to destruction. "We are cast down but not destroyed".

It was in Job's moments of solitude that he questioned God. He didn't air out his grievances with family and friends. He let them talk, but he kept the intimate details of how he was feeling to himself. There are many ways to process doubt and disappointment but publicly isn't always the best way. "For my thoughts are not your thoughts, neither are your ways my ways," declares the Lord. "As the heavens are higher than the earth, so are my ways higher than your ways and my thoughts than your thoughts". As you progress through the stages of emotion and move forward, do your best to keep an outlook of optimism, believing, *"this too shall pass"*. Use lessons learned from past mistakes, inner wisdom, and guidance to navigate your way and get back on course. If you need more formal guidelines, investigate established principles like the 12 Stages of Grief and seek spiritual insight to cope with disappointments.

IF IT KNOCKS YOU TO YOUR KNEES, YOU'D BETTER PRAY WHILE YOU'RE DOWN THERE

Don't panic if things don't go as planned. Hold fast to your faith and stay grounded in your values and beliefs. I know it's easier said than done when a challenge is staring you in the face. In the past, when situations knocked me to my knees, I lay on my face and prayed. Don't lose hope. Find peace in knowing that setbacks are often part of a bigger plan, and trust that everything will work out as it should. "The wicked have set a snare for me, but I have not strayed from Your precepts."

By handling setbacks with emotional control and diplomacy, you learn to master emotions and remain calm and composed. You manage your feelings, maintain a balanced demeanor, and address challenges with quiet strength and maturity. Manage setbacks by focusing on maintaining your emotional control and mental clarity. "God has not given you a spirit of fear, but of a sound mind, power, and love." Declare that over your life. When you're in a state of panic, you cannot hear guidance. Solutions are more difficult to ascertain.

Regaining your footing seems impossible. Make methodical moves. Stop. Pray. Ask for Guidance. Listen. Even when setbacks occur, keep looking for hope and inspiration. Quietly nurture your dreams and stay optimistic about what's ahead. Focus on finding ways to heal and renew your spirit, trusting that your journey has a purpose, no matter the challenges. Take a strategic approach to handling disappointments. Reflect on your options, think through your decisions, and carefully plan your next steps. Use this time to revisit your long-term goals and keep the details to yourself as much as possible. With a bit of discretion and foresight, you'll stay on track.

IDENTIFYING SELF-SABOTAGE & TAKING RESPONSIBILITY

Self-sabotage sneaks in when we let things like procrastination, lack of follow-through, or unhealed wounds hold us back from seizing opportunities. These habits can get in the way of our growth and success. Impulsive actions and careless words are also forms of self-sabotage, often creating conflicts and problems we don't need. Jumping to conclusions or getting caught up in gossip can damage relationships and shut down chances we might have otherwise had. Refusing to move on from past difficulties or neglecting to heal from past trauma will also hold you back. Dwelling on negative experiences instead of taking steps forward impedes your progress. Insecurity is another powerful self-sabotaging force that can prevent us from reaching our full potential because it causes us to:

- second-guess our abilities,
- avoid taking risks, and miss out on opportunities that could lead to growth and success,
- undermine our confidence,
- and hinder effective collaboration.

Insecurity distorts perception, leading to biased decisions and compromises that may not serve your best interests and may even lead to stress and overwhelm, making it difficult to lead with assurance and make decisive, balanced decisions. Overcoming insecurity is essential for maintaining stability, making fair decisions, and collaborating effectively. It allows you to take responsibility for your actions and contribute fully to group efforts without self-doubt or fear. Chronic insecurity can lead to a cycle of setbacks. Two steps forward ten steps back, so to speak. By keeping your struggles and setbacks private, you avoid getting stuck in resentment over past mistakes—both yours and others. This makes it easier to focus on the positives and learn from your experiences, which is key to growth and making positive changes. Fast, pray, and worship through your setbacks. The enemy is monitoring your life because they know that you are destined for greatness and the Kingdom of God will be glorified. Enemies will celebrate your losses, but they will not celebrate for long. God will elevate you. James 4:10 says, "Humble yourselves before the Lord, and he will lift you up.

Learn the power of being silent. Ask the Holy Spirit to give you guidance about who you should share with. Plead the blood of Jesus Christ over your home, family, career, and business- everything. Read Job 1:10 and then confess it over your life. "God has placed a hedge around me and my household and everything that I have. God has blessed the works of my hands". Be aware of ways that you may be self-sabotaging. This is so important. Use the following bullet points for future quick reference.

8 Ways We Self-Sabotage

1. **Succumbing to Fears and Anxieties**: Overthinking and dwelling on negative thoughts can paralyze us.
2. **Being Overly Idealistic**: Chasing unrealistic fantasies can lead to disappointment. Always dreaming but never planning or following through.
3. **Focusing Excessively on Material Success**: Prioritizing material possessions and external validation.
4. **Failing to Maintain Balance**: Overextending ourselves or becoming overly dependent can create imbalance.
5. **Allowing Emotional Imbalance**: Emotional instability and manipulation can disrupt our lives.
6. **Indecision and Fear of Risks**: Hesitation to make choices or act on plans can hinder progress.

7. **Neglecting Self-Care and Creativity**: Failing to nurture ourselves and our passions disconnects us from our potential.

8. **Over-Reliance on Logic**: Ignoring your gut instincts and intuition.

Understanding these potential self-sabotaging behaviors can help us recognize and address them, allowing us to create a more positive and productive path toward achieving our goals and dreams. "And let us not grow weary of doing good, for in due season we will reap if we do not give up."-Galatians 6:9. When we experience setbacks, patience becomes our greatest ally. Without it, we risk rushing into a quick fix without considering the consequences—or panicking and turning to people who may not have our best interests at heart. Talking about your dreams and plans, or even divulging your setbacks puts your dream at risk of being attacked by enemies- seen and unseen.

USE LEADERSHIP SKILLS TO NAVIGATE SETBACKs

Handle setbacks like a boss by staying calm, and focused, and turning challenges into opportunities for growth. Maintaining hope and inspiration requires patience and persistence. Trust in the process and stay focused on your long-term vision, even when you encounter obstacles along the way. Remember, setbacks are just stepping stones that bring you closer to your goals if you keep moving forward confidently and keep unnecessary people out of your business. Setbacks are literally part of the process.

MEMORY VERSE: PROVERBS 17: 28

Even fools are thought to be wise if they keep silent and discerning if they hold their tongues.

PRAYER

Lord, grant me the wisdom to guard my tongue and the discipline to remain silent when needed. Teach me to speak with discernment and to honor You in all my words and actions. In Jesus' name, Amen.

AFFIRMATION

I exercise wisdom by holding my tongue and practicing discernment. My words reflect thoughtfulness and honor to God.

MANTRA

"Silence reveals wisdom; discernment guides my words."

CHAPTER 7

STOP TELLING PEOPLE ABOUT YOUR GOALS

Stick with me, I know you may be thinking, "Ugh! I don't want to talk about goals let alone how to create goals". I completely understand. But remember, this will help increase your confidence and strengthen your resolve.

A great format to use is the SMART framework. S M A R T stands for specific, measurable, achievable, relevant, and time-sensitive (SMART). Once you learn this goal-setting skill, you will be less likely to need outside validation for your plans. Thereby allowing you to move in silence with stealth and confidence. You'll be able to focus on your objectives without being swayed by others' opinions or seeking constant reassurance. This internal confidence and self-reliance will enable you to pursue your goals more effectively, minimizing distractions and maximizing your chances of success.

Later we will discuss identifying strengths, weaknesses, opportunities, & threats. For now, let's talk about goals.

Goal creation has never been a practice I enjoyed. I once considered it tedious and time-consuming, but I have grown to respect and value its importance. And I now understand just how much I have limited my success, by avoiding this simple, yet vital first step, in the planning process. Trust me when I say, you will be glad you took the time to identify your goals.

Not taking the time to write measurable goals has stagnated me for years. Just take the time to do it and you will see the benefits. If this is too much for you to think about, skip this chapter and come back when you're ready, but please don't skip goal setting. Proverbs 21 verse 5: "The plans of the diligent lead to profit as surely as haste leads to poverty. "If this is not your thing, it can take a while to get the SMART goal-setting concept down, but once you get it, you won't want to create future goals without being SMART. Do you see what I did there? Again, you can draw on past experiences and lessons learned. By setting Specific, Measurable, Achievable, Relevant, and Time-bound goals, you can build on your past successes and memories, applying what you've learned to your current objectives. Maybe your goals weren't measurable in the past, so you didn't know if or when you accomplished your objective. Or perhaps your original goal wasn't relevant to your overall desired outcome.

Let's say you are on board with moving silently and you want to achieve a long-term goal of paying down your principal mortgage and using the equity to help purchase your dream home. I'm no expert in this, so I hope it gets the point across. An example, in my case, might be a SMART goal to increase my monthly mortgage payments by $500 over the next twelve months.

This goal is Specific (increase monthly mortgage payments), Measurable (by $500), Achievable (within my budget), Relevant (helps pay down principal faster), and Time-bound (over the next twelve months). By setting this SMART goal, I'll have a clear and actionable goal to pursue in achieving my long-term plan. SMART goals provide a structured and systematic approach to achieving your objectives. They bring a sense of order and discipline to your planning process, ensuring that your goals are well-defined and methodically pursued. Adhering to the SMART framework can help you stay focused, organized, and committed to your goals.

Setting goals helps you focus your intentions and efforts clearly and directly. With clear directions, I feel confident in my ability to move forward.

By setting goals, you create a roadmap that guides your actions and decisions, helping you maintain focus and motivation. With goal-setting strategies like these, you can harness your willpower and drive to achieve your objectives, ultimately leading to success and victory.

WRITE THE GOAL AND MAKE IT PLAIN.

Before any plan can be made, it's essential to know the goals. Using goal-setting techniques like SMART goal setting will give you a clear advantage when it comes to communicating your vision and purpose in writing. Habakkuk 2:2 reads: "And the Lord answered me, and said, 'Write the vision, and make it plain upon tables, that he may run that readeth it'."

Step into your role as the leader of your dreams. Embrace the spiritual principle of writing your vision and developing a clear plan that will allow the three divisions of yourself - body, soul, and spirit -to move forward with direction and purpose. You want your goals to align with your whole self. And that way when you act, you will do so with every fiber of your being.

IT'S DIFFICULT TO PLAN FORWARD PROGRESS WHEN YOU'RE CONSTANTLY LOOKING BACK.

To effectively transition your goals into a step-by-step plan, you may need to do some inner healing work first.

One vital area you want to reflect on is healing from past setbacks. Once promoted to governor, Joseph had to develop and execute a plan for managing Egypt's resources. Despite his past setbacks and betrayals, he did not allow hurt to interfere with reaching his goals.

Like Joseph, we must choose to move forward with hope and determination. Dwelling on past hurt and disappointment keeps us stuck. We must stay fixed on the goal, embrace change, and leave behind anything that can't go with us. Joseph likely thought of his family daily and felt the lingering pain of past wounds, but he didn't let those emotions derail his purpose. Instead, he remained focused and faithfully moved forward. We don't know much about his healing process or how he processed forgiveness, but we can learn from his obvious perseverance.

Forgiving helps us heal emotional wounds and negative *BS* clearing the path for strategic movement and thorough planning. Be bold and proactive in pursuing your vision. If He gave you the vision, He has your back, so don't be afraid to dream big.

God desires for us to succeed and fulfill the plans He has for us. As Jeremiah 29:11 reminds us, "For I know the plans I have for you," declares the Lord, "plans to prosper you and not to harm you, plans to give you hope and a future."

What God reveals to us is not always meant to be revealed to others, however, it can be tempting to share our goals with others prematurely.

Be mindful, as not everyone will support your vision—some may gossip, betray, or even work against your progress. Proverbs 4:23 cautions us, "Above all else, guard your heart, for everything you do flows from it," and this includes guarding your goals and intentions.

Instead, bring your goals before God in prayer, seeking His guidance through the Holy Spirit every step of the way (John 16:13). At the same time, be SMART about your goals—Specific, Measurable, Achievable, Relevant, and

Time-bound—to ensure you are purposeful and diligent in pursuing them. Proverbs 21:5: "The plans of the diligent lead to profit as surely as haste leads to poverty."

With prayer, wisdom, and God's guidance, you can move forward confidently toward success. Your plan is between you and God and the people he places on your path to journey with you. "Give ye not that which is holy to dogs, neither cast ye your pearls before swine, lest they tread them under their feet, and turning again, all to rent you." – Matthew 7:6

7 Kinds of Goals You can't share with just anyone

1. Don't share goals for a new business with coworkers.
2. Current financial status and future financial goals.
3. Opportunities for promotion.
4. Family goals and achievements.
5. Investments and business deals.
6. Relationship goals and desired outcomes.
7. Personal health goals.

When you fail to set goals, you plan to fail

If you doubt your ability to set goals and carry out a plan to completion, remember this: Proverbs 16:9, In their heart, humans plan their course, but the Lord establishes their steps." You are not doing this alone. God has promised to lead your steps, but you must begin by writing out your plans. It's time for you to put your dreams and goals on paper and give God something to work with. Fear can make you want to reach out for validation from others. Realize that this fear comes from negative beliefs like, "I can't do it," "I don't have what it takes" or "This goal is too big". It's all a bunch of *Negative B.S.* trying to get in the way of your confidence. Hopefully, this next chapter on planning can offer practical tips, techniques, and tools to help you overcome these fears, so you confidently develop your plan for moving forward.

MEMORY VERSE: PROVERBS 19:21 (AMPLIFIED)

Many plans are in a man's mind, but it is the Lord's purpose for him that will stand [be carried out].

PRAYER

Lord, I acknowledge that while I may have many plans, it is Your purpose that prevails. Help me to discern Your will in every situation and to trust in Your divine timing and plan for my life. Let Your purpose guide my steps and bring peace to my heart, knowing that Your way is always best. In Jesus' name, Amen.

AFFIRMATION

Though I have many plans, I trust in the Lord's purpose, for His plans for me will always prevail.

MANTRA

God's purpose prevails; His plan is perfect.

CHAPTER 8

STOP TELLING PEOPLE WHAT YOU'RE PLANNING

Joseph was ultimately promoted to governor of Egypt. As the governors of our own lives, we must learn to do as Luke 14:28 teaches us concerning planning or "sitting down and counting the cost." Maybe you davn't have a multi-million-dollar budget **yet**, but you do manage income and pay bills. You may not have employees, but you do interact with others in your social circle. If you're a student, you manage the stress of assignments, due dates, study requirements, and cohort relationships. If you have responsibilities of any kind, you should consider yourself a leader and take on the faith mindset of a governor like Joseph.

Successful planning and execution hinges on putting God first. Joseph listened to God and followed his lead which led to the effectiveness of his planning strategies. Whether you are a household of one or ten, always ensure that you and your house serve the Lord.

---

9 Important Elements of Successful Planning

---

1. Setting realistic goals
2. Analyzing your situation
3. Coming up with a strategy
4. Identifying and allocating resources
5. Creating a timeline
6. Implementing your plans
7. Monitoring & evaluating progress
8. Adjusting and adapting
9. Documenting what worked and what didn't

You set your goals in the previous chapter and now, before we set out on our journey, we want to take an honest look at where we are. Luke 14:28-30 says, "For which of you, intending to build a tower, sitteth not down first, and counteth the cost, whether he have sufficient to finish it? 29 Lest haply, after he hath laid the foundation, and is not able to finish it, all that behold it begin to mock him, 30 Saying, this man began to build and was not able to finish".

THE TRUTH WILL SET YOU FREE

When planning, be 100 percent honest with yourself about your situation. Your only competition is yourself. Start with what you have. Start where you are. I can tell you from experience that lying to yourself will only set you up for failure. Take a close look at your resources, constraints, and potential challenges. Consider my previous goal of paying down my mortgage principal. Let's say, two months into executing the mortgage paydown plan, I realize $500 is too much for my current budget and I haven't found a way to supplement my income. By acknowledging this, I give myself permission to reevaluate a strategy and come up with a more realistic amount for my budget in the meantime. If I can realistically only pay 100 dollars extra a month, that still making progress. Evaluating and adjusting is part of planning and execution. Continue moving forward and adjusting as you go. Remember Zechariah 4:10, "Do not despise small beginnings".

Every step forward is a win and even the small steps count. All that matters is that you are headed in the right direction.

This idea of reevaluating and readjusting highlights one of the benefits of planning in silence. The fewer people who know about your goal, the better. You'll be grateful that you didn't share your plans. Luke 14 Verse 30 warns us about the people who are waiting and watching for our plans to fail. Verse 30, "Saying, this man began to build and was not able to finish." Don't let this fear of people watchers discourage you. Remember, people are going to watch you anyway. So stay focused on your goals and plans, not the people who are watching. This is the stage where moving in silence and the elements of good planning skills come into play. When you hit a snag, there are less nosy naysayers to throw it in your face or gossip about it. You are free to stumble, fall, get back up, and forge ahead without any outside judgment or interference. This allows you to navigate challenges privately and stay focused on your journey, giving you the space to grow and succeed without added pressure or negativity. Plans change because circumstances change. That does not mean that you are a failure or that your dream is unattainable. It simply means, your plans need some adjustments. "Start where you are, use what you have, and do what you can." Arthur Ashe.

SWOT ANALYSIS

SWOT analysis-S-W-O-T- (stands for Strengths, Weaknesses, Opportunities, and Threats). This popular tool can be super helpful in planning as it helps you manage your weaknesses with wisdom and compassion and as well as it ensures your goals are realistic and well-thought-out. By clearly outlining your weaknesses and threats, a SWOT analysis allows you to come up with strategies to tackle these challenges and avoid getting overwhelmed. It sheds light on any uncertainties and hidden aspects of your goals, giving you clarity on what might otherwise be unclear. The SWOT analysis example that follows shows what it might look like for a busy mom who is aspiring to start her own business.

SWOT Scenario: Balancing A Family and a Home Business: Let's look at an example of a busy mom who is an aspiring entrepreneur. Using SWOT, we will identify strengths, weaknesses, opportunities, and threats. The first letter we will address is the letter S which stands for Strengths. Three key strengths have been identified:

1. **Organizational Skills**: She's great at managing her family's schedule, making her capable of handling multiple tasks efficiently.
2. **Support Network**: She has a supportive village who can help with childcare and household duties.
3. **Passion for the Business**: She is passionate about her new home business, giving her the motivation to succeed.

Next up, is the letter W, which stands for Weaknesses. Three weaknesses have been identified:

1. **Limited Time**: Balancing kids' activities, household chores, and the new business means time is limited.
2. **Lack of Experience**: She's new to running a business and might not have all the necessary skills yet.
3. **Stress Management**: Juggling so many responsibilities can be overwhelming and stressful.

The third letter, O, stands for Opportunities:

1. **Online Resources**: There are plenty of online courses and resources to learn business skills.
2. **Community Support**: Local mom groups or business networks can provide advice and support.

3. **Flexible Schedule**: Running a home business allows her to create a flexible schedule that fits her family's needs.

Finally, the last letter is T for Threats. Mom considers these three points as potential threats to her success:

1. **Unpredictable Family Needs**: Kids can get sick or need extra attention, requiring a change of plans.
2. **Financial Pressure**: The new business might take time to become profitable, adding financial stress.
3. **Competition**: There might be many other similar businesses, making it hard to stand out.

Now let's see how she can use SWOT to maximize opportunities and minimize the threats to her success:

First, let's look at the weaknesses and threats to see how she can better manage these aspects and improve her chances. Under weaknesses, she listed: limited time, lack of experience, and stress. To address the time management issue: She can create a detailed weekly schedule, allocating specific times for work, family, and self-care.

In my own life, I started by putting everything on a calendar to identify the blocks of time needed for tasks and who is responsible for them.

MANAGING TIME RESOURCES

We all have 24 hours in a day, but our days don't all look the same. If you feel like you are not as productive as you can be, take a few days and analyze how you spend the hours in your day, from waking to bedtime. Grab a planner that has the days broken down into hours. Write down what you are doing in each block of time. For example, from 11 pm to 6 am you may mark "sleep" and from 8 am to noon, you may mark "work". Be sure to write something for every time block, even if you feel that you did "nothing". Write it down and use the information later to identify potential free space in your schedule.

Time management has been a major turning point for me. Before, I was all over the place and wasting more time than I realized. Your time is valuable and as the saying goes, *time is money*. When you waste time, you waste money. Lack of experience is listed as another weakness. In this case, she could identify convenient ways to develop her skill set. Setting aside 30 minutes to an hour a day to learn new business skills will make a huge impact and quickly turn this weakness into a strength. I have increased my knowledge and skills by dedicating a small portion of my day to listening to videos and taking inexpensive online training certifications. There are professionals on every platform discussing their experiences and sharing valuable knowledge that you can take advantage of. Udemy is a favorite platform of mine for training and learning because it is affordable, and I've had much success with training and continued education that increased my skillset and added a bullet point or two to my resume. Thirdly, Mom in this scenario identified stress as a weakness. Let's talk about ways she could reduce stress. In this scenario, she could incorporate a few activities. Take a walk, knit (or in my case crochet), and meditate. Pray. Heck, take up kickboxing! Remember, your mental health is a priority.

I've learned from experience that managing my stress benefits not just me, but everyone around me.

If you need outside help to manage high anxiety or stress levels, you should seek it. Employers offer services as part of benefits packages and non-profits offer resources and information. It's that important. You deserve to live a well-balanced life. Do what you must to achieve that. If you need a break, take it. If you need to talk to someone, make the call. I can't stress that enough. Now that we've addressed the weaknesses, let's look at the threats. The first identified threat is "Unpredictable Family Needs". There is nothing more unpredictable than family.

A good strategy to mitigate the risk of unpredictable family issues is to have an emergency plan in place. Create a plan for when kids get sick or need extra attention. For example, research care providers, playgroups, etc. ahead of time, if you can, get buy-in from a trusted friend or family member to serve as emergency childcare. Give yourself a cushion in your schedule so that if something comes up unexpectedly, you still have wiggle room or flexibility with your deadlines. All of this can help mitigate the risk of being derailed by uncontrollable circumstances. These are simple examples. I know from experience that things will happen that are impossible to plan for. I'm here to tell you my friend, that those are the times when you roll with the punches. If you need to, put things on hold. And pick them up again when and if you can. Family comes before business. As Mary Kay Ash would say, "God first, family second, career third".

Practical strategies can help you manage any perceived weaknesses and threats. Remember, things will come up that are unavoidable and unexpected. Let's move forward using SWOT analysis to help Mom leverage her Strengths and Opportunities:

1. **Networking**: Joining local mom groups, coaching, or online business networks can provide support and potential business opportunities.

2. **Flexible Working Hours**: She can take advantage of the flexibility of running a home business to work during times that best fit her family's schedule, like early mornings or evenings.

3. **Delegating Tasks**: Mom has already identified that she has a supportive network. Here, she can leverage her organizational skills to delegate household tasks to other family members, freeing up time for her business.

By using a SWOT analysis, we can create a balanced approach to managing our roles and responsibilities while successfully pursuing our ambitions and goals.

Identifying your threats and weaknesses also helps you address any lurking fears and doubts, ensuring your planning is solid. Plus, analyzing before moving ahead highlights your strengths and opportunities, giving you direction on where to focus your energy to achieve your goals. You'll have no choice but to face and manage your weaknesses with courage and patience.

MANAGING TIMELINES AND MILESTONES

Develop a timeline or schedule that outlines when each task or activity will be completed. Set milestones to track progress and ensure that the plan stays on track. Remember, when you feel overwhelmed, try to break the task down into manageable action items. A bite-sized goal may be more realistic for your situation and help you achieve your milestones. Being thorough and reliable in your planning ensures that each step is well thought out and you avoid repeating steps. This way, you maintain steady progress. Keeping track of tasks and timelines will keep you disciplined in your approach and highlight the benefit of consistency and persistence. You will look back, see your steady progress, and be encouraged to continue.

Be patient and realistic. Remind yourself periodically, why you aspire to achieve this dream and why you were so passionate about it in the first place.

Again, you may find that adjustments are needed. That's okay. You are learning and growing every step of the way. Seek wisdom from experienced trustworthy people. Make the necessary adjustments and keep moving.

PLANNING AND RISK MANAGEMENT

As governor of your life, you must prepare for potential issues. This is known as risk management. It involves figuring out how likely these problems are and how much trouble they could cause, then making plans to handle or reduce these risks. Like Joseph, always put God first. Let him help you develop a strategy to minimize risks. Joseph strategically allocated resources so that there was a store of surplus grain during years of abundance. This minimized the risk of running out of food before the end of the famine. Proverbs 6:6-9 tells us to consider the ways of the ant. "Go to the ant, thou sluggard; Consider her ways, and be wise: Which having no chief, Overseer, or ruler, provideth her bread in the summer, And gathereth her food in the harvest. How long wilt thou sleep, O sluggard? When wilt thou arise out of thy sleep?" The ant teaches us to prepare. Look closely at your resources and honestly assess your situation. You want to be prepared for the unexpected so that you don't get caught off guard and your dreams and goals stay on track. It's like having roadside assistance for your car—nobody wants to break down but having help available if you do eases stress and makes getting back on the road much smoother.

Proverbs 22:3 speaks of the importance of foresight in planning. "A prudent man foreseeth the evil, and hideth himself: but the simple pass on, and are punished." Are there risks associated with your dreams? What are they? What is it that you fear could throw you off course? Don't be afraid to write them down and analyze them honestly. Doing so will help you plan for any potential problems.

PLANNING AND MINDSET

Your mindset is a major component. Your decisions will be impacted by your thoughts and beliefs. If you tend to fall into a lack mindset or fear-based mentality, you run the risk of quitting or giving up too soon. If you're afraid of planning, take a prayerful pause to check in with your core values and beliefs. Ask yourself some questions. Is there something internal that is stalling my progress? Am I self-sabotaging? Imagine this. You're trying to achieve a specific goal. You've tried several times, but each time, you face setbacks and eventually give up. Your idea is good, but you are always overthinking to the point of anxiety, so you give up too soon because you don't see results right away.

Maybe you want to write a book. However, you start but never complete a draft. Or you're an aspiring artist, but you don't practice work-life balance. You work your 9-5 to the point of exhaustion every day because you have a "work till you drop" belief system and your health suffers. As a result, you have no energy for your aspirations.

You can have an amazing idea, a clear vision, and a solid plan, but if you don't believe you are worthy, you might self-sabotage. Your negative beliefs could make you procrastinate. Fear of unworthiness or imposter syndrome can make you avoid networking opportunities or put in less effort to make beneficial connections. These behaviors, caused by your lack of alignment mind/soul/body-act as risk factors that get in the way of your success.

Imposter syndrome is when you feel like you're not good enough or don't truly deserve the accomplishments you've achieved. No matter how hard you have worked.

This can happen at any age. Your God-given talents come so naturally to you that you feel like you don't deserve to be celebrated for them. You feel like a fake and you worry that others will see you as a fake as well. The enemy wants you to think that you are doing everything alone and that you are weak, but with God, you are strong. "My grace is sufficient for you. My power is made perfect in weakness."
-2 Corinthians 12:9

Remember, in God's eyes, you are wonderfully made with a purpose (Psalm 139:14). God knows your heart and gifts better than anyone. Trust your Father in heaven. Ask Him to help you see that your worth isn't based on perfection or the approval of others.

You are not an imposter. You are a child of The Most High God. You are as real as they come. Build your self-confidence, adopt a more positive mindset, and fully commit to moving forward with intention and purpose—pray that God will help you to align your thoughts, behaviors, and beliefs. This soul-body-spirit alignment will significantly improve your chances of success.

This level of alignment doesn't happen overnight so don't get discouraged if you can't accomplish it in a day. Choose an area of spiritual growth to focus on and work in that area. If, for example, you have self-esteem challenges, like I had for many years, focus on that area. Search scriptures for self-esteem. Read them daily. Go to bed listening to them each night. Joshua 1:8, "This Book of the Law shall not depart from your mouth, but you shall meditate in it day and night, that you may observe to do according to all that is written in it. For then you will make your way prosperous, and then you will have good success."

Building your self-esteem will help you in other ways by boosting courage, motivating you to persevere, and shielding you against negative self-talk, self-deprecating behavior, and negative thought patterns.

Any Negative BS you've accumulated over time poses a risk not only to your ability to plan and execute successfully but also to your ability to believe in yourself. If you don't believe in yourself, you will seek outside validation, putting your entire plan of moving in silence at risk.

" For in him we live, and move, and have our being." Acts 17:28

One thing that can help you believe in yourself more is to remember that you are made in the image of your creator. It is in Him that you move and have your being. Remind yourself daily, that you are not alone in your quest. Though you are moving in silence, you are accompanied by the power of the Holy Spirit.

PLANNING AND MANAGING YOUR RESOURCES

As the governor of your own life, you want to become a good steward of your resources. When it comes to managing your finances, Negative BS about money can sabotage your plan's budget by causing you to spend recklessly, cut corners, or even lose out on investment opportunities. I speak from experience.

Resource Management. Spending on impulse will throw you and your plan execution off balance. Take the time to identify any emotional risk factors and address them ahead of time if possible or put a strategy in place to handle issues if they arise. If stress leads to overspending; make a note and consciously put a risk management strategy in place to mitigate the risk of emotional spending- like implementing a 24-hour waiting period before making any new purchases over a specified amount.

Time Management. Wasting time will make you lose opportunities and slow down your progress. If you know that a particular task in your plan puts you at risk of procrastinating, create a strategy to manage this stress. Say you need to make a call, but talking to strangers makes you nervous and you tend to put off making calls. Practicing conversations in the mirror or writing down key points before calls can help lessen stress and hopefully, you avoid missing deadlines and opportunities. If a task in your plan seems time-consuming, try breaking it down into smaller, more manageable steps, scheduling blocks of time for completing it, or seeking support from a mentor. Breaking the task into smaller steps may require more time but adjusting your dream's timeline is far better than giving up and quitting altogether.

A few months ago, I started a YouTube channel. I can't tell you the number of times I have started a video only to delete it. Being on camera isn't my thing, but I'm learning to face the fear and create strategies to help me do the most uncomfortable thing. I'm more comfortable writing than speaking on camera. I tried using notes and creating talking points, which has helped some. I'm not there yet and that's okay. Start where you are and find strategies that help you continue moving forward. By proactively addressing these emotional challenges, you can maintain your focus and keep your plan on track. What kind of strategies do you employ to keep yourself on track? I'd love to know.

PLANNING WITH INTEGRITY

The NIV version of Proverbs 11:3 states, "The integrity of the upright guides them, but the unfaithful are destroyed by their duplicity." Make sure the elements of your plans are fair to everyone. Integrity and ethical behavior are important to the longevity of your success. As the saying goes, how you get it is how you will lose it. The things you obtain dishonestly, you will likely lose quickly, and not only that, but you will also attract misfortune to yourself. Ill-gotten gains are not sustainable and can lead to negative consequences. It may appear that you are winning in the short term, but in the end, the endeavors will suffer.

"Be not deceived; God is not mocked: for whatsoever a man soweth, that shall he also reap." Galatians 6:7-9

Strive for balance in all aspects of your plan. Integrity and accountability are essential. Seize new opportunities and embrace your creative potential, but let your vision be driven by inspiration and innovative ideas, not greed and power.

"Be mindful of your intentions and never let greed, power, or financial gain drive your actions."

Act confidently, honorably, and decisively as a visionary leader during your planning process. Your ability to inspire others through your positive example will be crucial in achieving your vision. History has provided examples of many C EOs who fell victim and ultimately ended up in ruin. Trust that you can achieve your dreams and goals the right way by maintaining integrity through thoughtful planning and execution of your vision and goals.

MEMORY VERSE: PROVERBS 16:3 (AMPLIFIED)

Commit your works to the Lord [submit and trust them to Him], And your plans will succeed [if you respond to His will and guidance].

PRAYER

Father, I commit all my plans, work, and efforts to You. I trust You to guide me according to Your perfect will. Help me to align my desires with Your purpose and rely on Your wisdom in every decision. I know that as I surrender to You, my plans will succeed in ways that glorify You. In Jesus' name, Amen.

Affirmation

I commit my work to the Lord, trusting His guidance and timing, and He leads my plans to success according to His will.

Mantra

"I trust. I submit. I succeed—in God's will."

CHAPTER 9

PRAYERFULLY- RESPECTFULLY- STRATEGICALLY-MOVING IN SILENCE

Whew! We made it to the final chapter. I'm excited because this book has been months in the making and there has been one distraction after another. I hope you've gained some helpful tips and spiritual insights for your continued or newfound mission to move in silence. It's not for the weak; your inner circle may challenge you initially.

Ultimately, they will recognize and respect your decision as a wise and strategic move. If they don't, well, that's between them and God. Keep moving in love and let your actions speak for you.

Let them witness your faithful efforts as a testimony to God's ability to work through you to achieve His purposes.

Now that you know what's happening, you can never go back to oversharing again. Knowledge changes everything—it's like a light shining into places that once were hidden in darkness. From this day forward, be vigilant on your journey. Each choice you make, every dream you pursue, every step you take has the potential to draw attention, and while some attention can be uplifting, not all of it will be.

People are always listening and watching and so are monitoring spirits. Some people will celebrate you; others may seek to steal, kill, and destroy.

Remember, the enemy operates subtly, playing on your emotions, distracting, and triggering you through unhealed traumas. This is why you cannot tell everyone everything.

Deliver Me From Talking Too Much!

Not every listener has pure intentions, and not every conversation is just an innocent exchange. Sharing too much can leave your endeavors vulnerable to negativity.

By moving in silence, you gain power. Silence becomes your armor, shielding you from those who have evil intentions. You don't owe anyone an explanation for your goals, your dreams, or the purpose God has set in your heart. This journey of a dreamer is sacred, personal, and divinely appointed. It requires you to be led by the Holy Spirit and discernment. Keep your goals close to your vest, as they say. Only share intimate details sparingly. Your actions will speak louder than words.

In this season of silence, cultivate a deeper connection with God. Seek His guidance and let Him bring the right connections and support with equally yoked friends and partners. Again, this is not for you to become a hermit and hide under a rock. This is about practicing discernment, finding peace in solitude, and being intentional with whom you share your business.

Silence in this sense, is not toxic isolation—it's protection. It's giving you space to grow, reflect, and allow God to work in you without the noise of external opinions or interference.

This season is about nurturing what God has planted within you, away from the distractions and influences that can pull you off course. It's about moving wisely, discerning intentions, and keeping your plans primarily between you and God until they're ready to be revealed. By choosing to move in silence, you give God room to guide your steps without unnecessary noise. It's not about hiding in fear from people, but about allowing Him to hide you under his wings and present you in His timing. This journey requires patience and trust—trust that what God has for you is meant to be yours.

Embrace the silence as a powerful and sacred space where God prepares you for what's to come and reveals truths about people that you've never seen- or chose to ignore in the past.

Through prayer and faith, you will find the strength to remain focused and the courage to move forward quietly, confidently, and under the protection of His grace. Moving forward, you must reframe how you see setbacks.

They are opportunities to learn lessons, reflect, reevaluate, and come back stronger. Progress is progress- fast or slow. Be gentle with yourself. As you encounter bumps, hiccups, and challenges, resist the temptation to tell the world your problems. You should not be surprised when people begin to fall away from your life. Their season may have come to an end. These people are like leaves that must fall away when the season changes. If they fall away, trust God that new leaves will grow. The people who remain long-term become a part of your root system. They are nurturing and supportive, helping you to remain anchored as you continue to expand and grow. Your goals, intentions, and dreams may not always match the Leaf people, but the roots will be with you for a lifetime. It may hurt when some people's nefarious intentions are exposed. You're human and that is normal. Do not harbor resentment or stoop to the lower level of revenge. Pray for them. Pray for yourself. Forgive them. Forgive yourself.

"Beware of false prophets, who come to you in sheep's clothing, but inwardly they are ravenous wolves. 16 You will know them by their fruits." -Matthew 7:15

If you're having trouble discerning, remember that envy, jealousy, anger, resentment, and dishonesty, are all signs of an unequally yoked person who is not meant to remain in your circle. They may have an assignment, for a time, to teach you and them valuable lessons on loyalty, trust, self-worth, and discernment. Joseph didn't discern his brother's intentions. Perhaps he was naïve and boastful. His brothers failed to discern Joseph's purpose. Perhaps, they were insecure and envious. Still, God worked through all of them to achieve His purpose and plan. The brothers thought they were hurting Joseph by throwing him into the pit, but they helped further the plan to place Joseph in a position to one day help his entire family.

If someone has rejected or pushed you away, know it will all work together for the bigger plan. If you have been led to walk away, but you don't understand why, just be obedient. People will label you crazy but trust your discernment and go where the Holy Spirit leads you. Some people cannot follow you on your journey, and the reasons won't always be clear.

A season of solitude is sometimes needed for inner healing and introspection before moving forward with any plans. Solitary seasons are good times to reflect and heal, especially after experiencing a major life change. There will also be times when God will hide you for your benefit. "For in the day of trouble he will keep me safe in his dwelling; he will hide me in the shelter of his sacred tent and set me high upon a rock." -Psalm 27:5

Try always to remain balanced and self-aware. If you find that you are isolating yourself and it begins to feel like the walls are closing in or you're depressed, this may be a sign of something deeper and you should seek outside guidance from a trusted professional.

THEY MAY SLEEP ON YOU, BUT GOD IS ALWAYS AWAKE

Psalm 21:4 says He will never sleep nor slumber. When it gets dark for you on this journey, remember that God is always awake. Moving in silence is your time to walk by faith, not sight. Careful not to misjudge others who are not on this path with you. Do not talk down on them or take hasty action against them. Moving in silence doesn't make you better. It just means you are on a different path. This brings up the topic of patience. Do your research on the path that you are choosing. Whatever this dream or goal is that you are pursuing, study it. Study what successful others have done before you. Learn from their mistakes and their experiences. Then be patient with yourself. What takes someone else a few months may take another person a few years and a strong desire to succeed, regardless of obstacles, requires patience and persistence, but you can achieve it. "You will not be tempted or tried above what you can accomplish." If your plan is God-centered, all of heaven will have your back. There may be many detours, but patience gives you a major advantage.

If there is a delay, it may be God trying to teach you something before you reach your destination that will help you achieve greatly when you get there.

Don't allow the projections of others to deter you from your goals. Their doubts, fears, or limitations do not determine your success. People project their insecurities or past failures onto others, but you don't have to be their movie screen. Remember, your vision was given to you for a reason—it's uniquely yours and meant for you to pursue. Keep moving forward with faith, knowing that only you and God truly know the potential within you.

Negative Belief Systems BS

It's not all about what is going on outside of you. There is the case of self-sabotage, and it must be addressed the minute it rears its ugly head. Look in the mirror, and identify the issue, whether it be negative belief systems, fear, unworthiness, low self-esteem, a lack mindset, or unhealed trauma- you must deal with it. Never be afraid to sit with yourself and question why you believe what you do and how it impacts the decisions that you make. Your life reflects the decisions that you've made, so you need to understand why you're making those decisions. "In all of your getting, get a good understanding". Give yourself grace. You cannot control every aspect of your life. There is a quote that talks about when we plan, God laughs. When something does not go as planned, that is not the time to give up. Daily, identify self-sabotage and break free from its unhealthy patterns, addictions, or behaviors that are holding you back. Avoid the temptation to seek validation from others, as it can create a dependency on external approval and hold you back. Often, the urge to overshare stems from a desire for validation. While healing takes time, freeing yourself from the need for others' approval is a powerful step forward.

INCLUDE GOD IN YOUR PLANS AND GOALS

God must be at the center of your plans. Implement planning and goal-setting strategies to have a practical step-by-step guide at your fingertips. Take time to SWOT your goals. List strengths, weaknesses, opportunities, and perceived threats to get clear. Journal and take notes through the different stages. This helps document the experience and knowledge gathered along the way.

Draw strength and learn lessons from overcoming setbacks and challenges. The setback is part of the journey. You won't just shoot forward in life without having to fall back a time or two, or three, or four. Acknowledge the battles you've faced but acknowledge more so how much you grow.

After each setback, give yourself time to catch your breath, get back on track, and move forward with passion and purpose. Keep pressing forward, even when obstacles arise, trusting in God's strength that is made perfect in your time of weakness. Make thoughtful decisions with integrity to ensure you're in harmony with your body, soul, and spirit.

DON'T IGNORE WARNING SIGNS

In Joseph's case, I imagine his brothers must have rolled their eyes, grunted, and probably even called him crazy, but he still kept talking. Don't ignore signs that someone may be holding secret animosity. We discussed some of the body language earlier like, huffing, puffing, grunting, and glaring. All of these are signs of discomfort and irritation. Whether they are irritated with you, is something for you to discern, but do not ignore your gut.

Reign in your negative self-talk, self-hatred, and criticism. Notice if you happen to be criticizing yourself too harshly, hesitating when opportunities come your way, or doing things that hold you back from success.

When you can recognize this in yourself and do something about it, you have truly matured and evolved. Inner battles can impact many parts of your life, like relationships and career goals, making it hard to see the opportunities ahead. To overcome this self-sabotage, it's important to understand yourself. No one should know better what makes you tick than you. No one should know better what triggers you, than you do. And when you do uncover these things about yourself, show yourself some kindness, and actively work towards positive changes and spiritual growth.

BLESSED TO BE A BLESSING

Galatians 6:7 reminds us, 'Do not be deceived: God cannot be mocked. A man reaps what he sows. The biblical principle of sowing and reaping states, that whatever you plant, you will ultimately harvest. Don't let this journey be all about moving in silence so that you can succeed and then leave everyone else in the dust. Once you "make it" to your goal, give back. Become a trusted member of someone's network. As we receive guidance and assistance in achieving our dreams, we should consider giving back when and where we can- with discernment. Giving back sows harmony and produces relationships with equal reciprocity. Think of it as sowing and reaping a harvest. (Caution- don't forget the opportunistic personality types we discussed who seek to benefit from your success for selfish gain. Avoid them. Keep them out of your business and your blessings.). As you elevate from faith to faith and glory to glory, be a blessing. Give back, as you are guided, to show your appreciation and gratitude to God. Ultimately, Joseph was blessed to be a blessing, not only to Potiphar, but to his family. We too are blessed to be a blessing.

FOCUS ON THE GOALS, NOT THE TROLLS

Many people have eyes on you. They all have their reasons. There is a spectrum of good and evil. On the one side there are people with perfectly harmless intentions, while on the opposite end, there are those who are unhealed and hurtful. They've opened themselves to spirits of jealousy, envy, and mischievous deeds. These people can be any of us. Just be sure you don't become one of them, but if you do, correct yourself, immediately, so God won't have to do it for you. God doesn't play about His children, and He won't let us play with them either. "To whom much is given, much is required." Luke 12:48.

Just like you are on a mission to live out your purpose, someone else is on a mission to stop you from doing so.

DISCERNMENT IS A GIFT. USE IT.

I've hammered this topic of discernment, but it is so important. Some people naturally have discernment, others have not yet cultivated theirs. Trust your gut and with each experience think about what you learned from it. Building your discernment will help you to identify the intentions of others early to avoid problems. Please don't ignore when a person or circumstance makes you feel suspicious. Ask yourself why. Discernment doesn't hit you like a ton of bricks. It is subtle, silent, and quiet. It is the subtle knowing that something isn't right.

SETBACKS CAN BE SETUPS FOR SUCCESS

The Holy Spirit will guide you when you need instruction and direction as well as comfort you when you encounter setbacks and disappointments because you will. No journey to purpose is easy nor is the road to realizing dreams a smooth ride. That is why so few stick with it. If you're reading this, you are one of the few who have the determination to try. Believe that if God gave you this desire, He has also given you spiritual gifts to assist you along the way. You understand now that moving in silence is a strategy. It's not a petty way to get back at anyone or an outward display of arrogance. Instead, it's a deliberate approach to protect your goals and progress, allowing you to grow without unnecessary interference.

RESPECTFULLY MOVING IN SILENCE

My intentions for this book were to provide you with a guide to help you understand and navigate moving in silence. Not to make you paranoid or angry. I hope that you have a greater sense of urgency when it comes to nurturing and protecting your dreams. You have every right to protect your private business. Do so with pure intentions, respectfully, without creating chaos. "God is not the author of confusion but of peace". Silently withdraw when you can. When you cannot withdraw in silence, state your position clearly and stand on it. Then move on with your plans.

KEEPING YOUR PLANS TO YOURSELF

Ephesians 3:7: A time to tear and a time to mend, a time to be silent and a time to speak.

You must protect your plans, especially in the beginning. The wrong influences can derail the best-laid plans. A purpose team of equally yoked believers like the ones discussed in the previous chapters is your outlet for sharing, venting, and bouncing ideas off. Important dreams and goals are not for the ears of the unequally yoked. Equally yoked people are less likely to share your plans with others. They will respect your ideas and protect them from being stolen or misused. In competitive environments and settings where unique ideas are coveted, a high level of discretion should be used. Innovation makes money and puts companies in a great position to be successful. As a CEO of your life, you must protect your ideas as companies do. They put in place things like intellectual patents, trademarks, and copyrights to name a few. On a personal level, you have the same tools available. Just as a non-disclosure or patent is important to a business, so is discretion important to you. If you haven't already, pray and ask God to send you equally yoked believers to support your goals. Once you cultivate a safe environment where you can share your plans and progress without fear of judgment or betrayal, the people you confide in should prove to be loyal. This does not mean they act as enablers, ignoring issues and making decisions based on fantasy but on wisdom, faith, and integrity concerning the plan that you have been given to carry out. Network with those whose faith aligns with your own. These are your purpose team members. They are heavenly sent brothers and sisters or

Purpose Partners. They too are people of purpose. They can be trusted with the private details of your personal life and business. This group prays for you in your absence. They share in your accomplishments and support you in your seasons of setbacks. They keep you honest. Tell you when you are wrong, but always make you feel supported and loved.

THE SPIRIT OF GOD MOVED

If you feel stagnant, know this; your dream is like a seed. A seed goes through phases after it is planted. Just because you can't see what's happening, doesn't mean God isn't doing something invisible to your eye. This spiritual element of mystery is why people around you lack clarity of His plans for your life. Sometimes it is that you are being protected. Don't beat yourself up over delays or worse give up completely. Instead, pray, re-strategize, and accept that you are being divinely detoured. Remember who you are. You are created in His image. You too, are a creator. Have faith in the dream God planted inside you. People can't see God's intentions for you. **You see, our God moves in silence, and He also moves in the dark.** "And the earth was without form and void, and darkness was upon the face of the deep: and the Spirit of *God moved* upon the face of the waters." Genesis 1:2

The Spirit of God has been moving in silence since the beginning. He is moving in silence, on your behalf, right now. Do not lose hope. Don't fear what man can do to you. "Greater is He that is in you than he that is in the world." You are made in the image of God, so move like God. Move in silence. Use your spiritual discernment to move in the dark. "Walk by faith, not by sight." The power has been given to you to move mountains.

MEMORY VERSE: 1 PETER 4:10-11 (NIV)

"Each of you should use whatever gift you have received to serve others, as faithful stewards of God's grace in its various forms. If anyone speaks, they should do so as one who speaks the very words of God. If anyone serves, they should do so with the strength God provides, so that in all things God may be praised through Jesus Christ. To Him be the glory and the power forever and ever. Amen"

PRAYER

Lord, thank You for the gifts You have entrusted to me. Help me to use them faithfully to serve others and bring You glory. May my words and actions reflect Your grace, and may Your strength guide me in all I do. To You be all glory and power forever. In Jesus' name, Amen.

AFFIRMATION

I am a faithful steward of God's grace. I use my gifts to serve others with His strength, and in all things, my life brings glory to God through Jesus Christ.

MANTRA

"My gifts serve His glory; His strength carries me forward."

Thank You

Thank you for spending this time with me. I send you love and prayers for a blessed journey as you pursue your dreams, goals, and purpose. I hope you received something from this message that helps you on your journey. Blessings to you and yours!

If you find something useful in this title, I ask that you would do me a favor. Join my email list and leave a comment on Amazon to tell me about it. I'd love to know. Thank you, family. See you next time.

GREAT WAYS TO USE THIS BOOK

Group/Setting	Purpose/How to Use the Book
Book Club	Facilitate group discussions on key themes and applications from the book.
Prayer Group	Use as a guide for scripture-based prayers and discussions on spiritual growth.
Women's Meeting	Focus on topics of empowerment, faith, and personal development relevant to women.
Men's Meeting	Explore themes of leadership, faith, and overcoming challenges from a Christian perspective.
Christian Business Network	Provide insights on faith-driven principles for success and integrity in business.
Small Group Bible Study	Use chapters or sections as weekly study material paired with scripture.
Sunday School Class	Integrate lessons from the book into class discussions to deepen understanding of biblical principles.
Youth Group Meeting	Encourage discussions on faith, self-esteem, and purpose tailored to young adults.
Personal Devotional	Read as a daily guide for prayer, reflection, and spiritual growth.
Retreat or Workshop	Use as a foundational resource for breakout sessions or personal growth activities.

SECTION II

CHAPTER DISCUSSION QUESTIONS

CHAPTER 1 DISCUSSION QUESTIONS

1. Why is discretion important when working toward your dreams? How can keeping plans private enhance your chances of success?
2. How does moving in silence protect you from external negativity or criticism? In what ways can this approach help maintain focus and motivation?
3. What are some potential risks of oversharing your dreams and aspirations with others? How can being too open make you vulnerable to discouragement or sabotage?
4. How can practicing discretion foster a sense of inner strength and confidence? In what ways does it empower you to take control of your narrative and actions?
5. Can you identify situations where being discreet might be challenging? How can you balance transparency with the wisdom of moving in silence?

CHAPTER 2 DISCUSSION QUESTIONS

1. Why do you think individuals spy on others in silence? Do their motivations stem from curiosity, control, jealousy, or something else?

2. How does the silent observation of others impact our behavior or decision-making? Can being aware of such scrutiny change how you act?

3. In what ways can silent observers influence your life without you knowing? Are there any signs or cues that might reveal their presence?

4. Why do some people feel the need to monitor others rather than engage openly? What does this behavior say about their own insecurities or desires?

5. How can you protect yourself from the negative influence of silent watchers or spies? What strategies can you use to maintain your privacy and peace of mind?

CHAPTER 3 DISCUSSION QUESTIONS

1. How can we recognize when our dreams are under spiritual attack? What signs or patterns might indicate the enemy's influence?

2. What strategies does the enemy commonly use to undermine our faith and confidence in pursuing God-given dreams? How can we counteract these tactics?

3. In what ways can prayer, scripture, and spiritual discernment help us defend against the enemy's attempts to steal, kill, and destroy our aspirations?

4. How does maintaining a strong relationship with God and a supportive faith community help protect us from spiritual attacks on our dreams and goals?

5. What role does perseverance play in overcoming spiritual attacks? How can we remain steadfast in pursuing our God-given purpose despite challenges?

CHAPTER 4 DISCUSSION QUESTIONS

1. How can we recognize when someone is projecting their insecurities or negative emotions onto us, and what are effective ways to respond?

2. In what ways do you think projecting energy (positive or negative) onto others can impact relationships, both personal and professional?

3. Can the act of projection be unconscious, and if so, how can individuals become more aware of when they are projecting onto others?

4. What role does empathy play in understanding and managing energy projections from others? How can setting healthy boundaries help?

5. How can societal norms and expectations influence the ways people project their energy onto others? What are some examples where this happens?

CHAPTER 5 DISCUSSION QUESTIONS

1. Why is it important to build a supportive and loyal network of fellow believers when pursuing God-given dreams? How can this network help us stay focused on our purpose?

2. What qualities should we look for in "purpose team" members who will walk alongside us in faith as we pursue our calling?

3. How can the right network support us through trials and spiritual attacks, helping us keep our faith and focus while still pursuing our dreams with discernment?

4. What are the potential dangers of depending too much on others for guidance, and how can we balance seeking counsel from our network with walking by faith and trusting in God's timing?

5. Can you think of examples where someone's network played a key role in their success? What spiritual lessons can be drawn from their approach?

CHAPTER 6 DISCUSSION QUESTIONS

1. What are some common setbacks people encounter when pursuing their dreams, and how can these challenges serve as opportunities for growth and learning?

2. How do you stay motivated and maintain focus on your goals after experiencing a setback? What strategies help you regain momentum and move forward?

3. In what ways can setbacks change your approach or perspective on your dreams, and how can this be beneficial in the long run?

4. How important is resilience in the pursuit of dreams, and how can setbacks strengthen your ability to adapt and continue toward your goals?

5. Can you share a personal experience of overcoming a significant setback while pursuing a goal? What lessons did you learn, and how did it impact your journey forward?

CHAPTER 7 DISCUSSION QUESTIONS

1. How can setting specific, measurable goals help you stay on track with your dream and avoid distractions along the way?

2. How can sharing your goals too early with others potentially open the door to sabotage or negative energy,

3. What role does self-doubt play in sabotaging goals, and how can one develop a mindset that supports the nurturing and protection of their goals?

4. How can identifying weaknesses and opportunities help further your progress as you plan for success?

5. What are some examples of practices or habits that can help maintain focus and protect your goals from external sabotage?

CHAPTER 8 DISCUSSION QUESTIONS

1. In what ways can breaking your plan down into manageable, actionable steps help you overcome feelings of overwhelm or uncertainty?

2. Can you think of examples where strategic planning was crucial to someone's success, and how can you apply those lessons to the pursuit of your own goals?

3. Why is it important to develop a clear plan for your dreams, and how can thoughtful planning help you stay focused and achieve better results than just going with the flow?

4. What role does reflection and careful consideration play in creating a strategic plan for your goals?

5. How can reflection help you stay aligned with your overall vision?

CHAPTER 9 DISCUSSION QUESTIONS

1. Why is it important to invest in other people's dreams, even before you have achieved your own, and how is this mindset beneficial?

2. How can helping others pursue their dreams create a positive ripple effect in your own journey toward success?

3. What are some practical ways to give back to others—whether through mentorship, resources, or encouragement—without seeking recognition?

4. How can building a culture of mutual support and encouragement contribute to long-term success for everyone involved?

5. Can you think of examples where someone's generosity and willingness to help others with their dreams ultimately benefited their own journey? What lessons can be learned from their story?

Note: Section 3, Study Tables, is available for e-books and paperback only. Audiobooks do not read the charts in this section.

Thank you.

SECTION III

HELPFUL STUDY

TABLES

Guarding Your Name and Character: Biblical Topics and Scriptures

Topic	Insight	Scripture Reference
The Power of Words	Words hold power to uplift or destroy; choose them wisely.	*Proverbs 18:21* – "The tongue has the power of life and death."
Speaking Ill of Others	Slandering others is condemned by God.	*James 4:11* – "Do not speak evil against one another, brothers."
God's Protection of Your Name	God will defend your reputation when wronged.	*Isaiah 54:17* – "No weapon formed against you shall prosper, and every tongue which rises against you in judgment You shall condemn."
The Sin of Gossip	Gossip causes division and harm among people.	*Proverbs 16:28* – "A perverse person stirs up conflict, and a gossip separates close friends."
Bearing False Witness	Lying about someone's character is sinful and damaging.	*Exodus 20:16* – "You shall not give false testimony against your neighbor."
Trusting God Amid Slander	God will vindicate you when others attack your character.	*Psalm 37:6* – "He will make your righteousness shine like the dawn, your justice like the noonday sun."
Refraining from Retaliation	Do not repay evil with evil but leave room for God's justice.	*Romans 12:19* – "Do not take revenge, my dear friends, but leave room for God's wrath."
Guarding Against Slander	Protect others' reputations by refusing to spread lies.	*Ephesians 4:29* – "Do not let any unwholesome talk come out of your mouths, but only what is helpful for building others up."
The Impact of Character Assassination	God warns against tearing down others for personal gain or spite.	*Proverbs 11:9* – "With their mouths the godless destroy their neighbors."
Maintaining Integrity	Your actions should reflect Christ, even when maligned.	*1 Peter 2:12* – "Live such good lives among the pagans that... they may see your good deeds and glorify God."
God's Knowledge of the Heart	God knows the truth about your character, regardless of others' words.	*1 Samuel 16:7* – "The Lord does not look at the things people look at."
Blessing Those Who Curse You	Show love and grace to those who speak against you.	*Luke 6:28* – "Bless those who curse you, pray for those who mistreat you."

Deliver Me From Talking Too Much!

The Power of the Tongue and Words: A Biblical Perspective

Topic	Insight	Scripture Reference
Words Have Power	Words can build up or tear down.	*Proverbs 18:21* – "The tongue has the power of life and death."
Speak with Wisdom	Wise words bring healing and life.	*Proverbs 15:4* – "The soothing tongue is a tree of life."
Guard Your Speech	Being mindful of what we say prevents harm.	*Psalm 141:3* – "Set a guard over my mouth, Lord; keep watch over the door of my lips."
Encourage Others	Uplifting words strengthen and encourage.	*Ephesians 4:29* – "Do not let any unwholesome talk come out of your mouths, but only what is helpful for building others up."
Avoid Gossip and Slander	Gossip creates division and harms relationships.	*Proverbs 16:28* – "A perverse person stirs up conflict, and a gossip separates close friends."
Speak Truth in Love	Words should be truthful and motivated by love.	*Ephesians 4:15* – "Speaking the truth in love, we will grow to become in every respect the mature body of Christ."
Be Slow to Speak	Listening first prevents careless words.	*James 1:19* – "Everyone should be quick to listen, slow to speak, and slow to become angry."
Words Reflect the Heart	Our speech reveals the condition of our hearts.	*Matthew 12:34* – "For the mouth speaks what the heart is full of."
Control the Tongue	The tongue, though small, has great influence.	*James 3:5* – "Likewise, the tongue is a small part of the body, but it makes great boasts."
Speak with Kindness	Kind words bless both the speaker and the listener.	*Proverbs 16:24* – "Gracious words are a honeycomb, sweet to the soul and healing to the bones."

Move In Silence: Lessons From the Story of Joseph

Lesson	Insight	Scripture Reference
God gives us dreams.	God plants divine dreams in our hearts for a purpose.	*Genesis 37:5-7* – "Joseph had a dream, and when he told it to his brothers, they hated him all the more."
Keep your dreams silent.	Not everyone is ready to hear or support your vision.	*Genesis 37:9-10* – "He told his father as well, and his father rebuked him."
Pay attention to people's reactions.	Responses to your vision reveal who is for you and against you.	*Genesis 37:11* – "His brothers were jealous of him, but his father kept the matter in mind."
Discern people's intentions.	Not everyone around you has your best interests at heart.	*Genesis 37:18-20* – "Here comes that dreamer! Come now, let's kill him."
Never give up on your dreams.	God's promises may take time, but they will come to pass.	*Habakkuk 2:3* – "Though it linger, wait for it; it will certainly come and will not delay."
God is faithful.	Even in adversity, God's plan prevails.	*Genesis 50:20* – "You intended to harm me, but God intended it for good."

Lesson	Insight	Scripture Reference
God will lead you.	He provides direction through challenges.	*Proverbs 3:5-6* – "Trust in the Lord with all your heart... He will make your paths straight."
God will protect you.	His hand shields you from ultimate harm.	*Psalm 121:7-8* – "The Lord will keep you from all harm—He will watch over your life."
God will help you plan.	Strategic preparation is part of fulfilling your destiny.	*Genesis 41:34-36* – Joseph advises Pharaoh on storing food during the famine.
Forgiveness is healing.	Letting go of bitterness frees you and aligns you with God's will.	*Genesis 50:17-21* – Joseph forgives his brothers for selling him into slavery.
People will betray you.	Betrayal may come even from those closest to you.	*Genesis 37:28* – "They sold him for twenty shekels of silver to the Ishmaelites."
Don't self-sabotage your dreams.	Stay faithful to God, even in temptation and trials.	*Genesis 39:9* – "How then could I do such a wicked thing and sin against God?"

KNOWING THE HOLY SPIRIT

Topic	Description	Key Scriptures
Who is the Holy Spirit	The Holy Spirit is God's Spirit, present to empower, comfort, and guide believers.	- John 14:26 - 2 Corinthians 3:17 - Acts 2:38
Your Comforter	The Holy Spirit provides comfort in times of trouble, grief, or uncertainty.	- John 14:16-17 - Romans 8:26-27 - Psalm 34:18
Your Guide	The Holy Spirit leads believers into all truth and reveals God's will.	- John 16:13 - Romans 8:14 - Isaiah 30:21
Your Power	The Holy Spirit equips believers with strength and boldness to live for God.	- Acts 1:8 - Ephesians 3:16 - Zechariah 4:6
Your Teacher	The Holy Spirit helps believers understand and apply God's Word.	- John 14:26 - 1 Corinthians 2:10-12 - 2 Timothy 3:16
Your Mentor	The Holy Spirit develops character and helps believers grow in their faith.	- Galatians 5:22-23 - Philippians 1:6 - 2 Corinthians 3:18
The Voice of God	The Holy Spirit speaks to believers, guiding them in their walk with God.	- Acts 13:2 - Hebrews 3:7-8 - 1 Kings 19:12

Discernment Scripture	Reference
"If any of you lacks wisdom, you should ask God, who gives generously to all without finding fault, and it will be given to you."	*James 1:5*
"Do not conform to the pattern of this world, but be transformed by the renewing of your mind. Then you will be able to test and approve what God's will is—his good, pleasing and perfect will."	*Romans 12:2*
"For the word of God is alive and active. Sharper than any double-edged sword, it penetrates even to dividing soul and spirit, joints and marrow; it judges the thoughts and attitudes of the heart."	*Hebrews 4:12*
"Test all things; hold fast to what is good."	*1 Thessalonians 5:21*

Deliver Me From Talking Too Much!

Topic	Bible Verse	Scripture Reference
Know Your Strengths	"I can do all things through Christ who strengthens me."	Philippians 4:13 (NKJV)
Know Your Weaknesses	"But he said to me, 'My grace is sufficient for you, for my power is made perfect in weakness.' Therefore I will boast all the more gladly of my weaknesses..."	2 Corinthians 12:9 (ESV)
Seek Opportunities	"Make the most of every opportunity, because the days are evil."	Ephesians 5:16 (NIV)
Identify Threats	"Be sober-minded; be watchful. Your adversary the devil prowls around like a roaring lion, seeking someone to devour."	1 Peter 5:8 (ESV)

Topic	Scripture
Having a Vision	*Proverbs 29:18* – "Where there is no vision, the people perish: but he that keepeth the law, happy is he."
Developing Plans	*Proverbs 16:3* – "Commit to the Lord whatever you do, and he will establish your plans."
Evaluating Your Circumstances	*Luke 14:28* – "Suppose one of you wants to build a tower. Won't you first sit down and estimate the cost?"
Writing Your Goals	*Habakkuk 2:2* – "Write the vision; make it plain on tablets, so he may run who reads it."
Considering Risks	*Proverbs 22:3* – "The prudent see danger and take refuge, but the simple keep going and pay the penalty."
Handling Setbacks	*James 1:2-4* – "Consider it pure joy, my brothers and sisters, whenever you face trials of many kinds, because you know that the testing of your faith produces perseverance."
Seeking Wise Counsel	*Proverbs 15:22* – "Plans fail for lack of counsel, but with many advisers they succeed."
Importance of Giving Back	*Acts 20:35* – "It is more blessed to give than to receive."
Staying the Course	*Galatians 6:9* – "Let us not become weary in doing good, for at the proper time we will reap a harvest if we do not give up."

Deliver Me From Talking Too Much!

Topic	Scripture
Increase Your Confidence	*Philippians 4:13* – "I can do all things through Christ who strengthens me."
Improve Your Self-Esteem	*Psalm 139:14* – "I praise you because I am fearfully and wonderfully made; your works are wonderful."
Heal Relationships	*Ephesians 4:32* – "Be kind and compassionate to one another, forgiving each other, just as in Christ God forgave you."
Learn to Forgive	*Matthew 6:14* – "For if you forgive other people when they sin against you, your heavenly Father will also forgive you."
Overcome Hurt	*Psalm 147:3* – "He heals the brokenhearted and binds up their wounds."
Empower Yourself	*2 Timothy 1:7* – "For the Spirit God gave us does not make us timid, but gives us power, love, and self-discipline."
Trust God for Help	*Proverbs 3:5-6* – "Trust in the Lord with all your heart and lean not on your own understanding; in all your ways submit to him, and he will make your paths straight."
Stand Firm on God's Promises	*2 Corinthians 1:20* – "For no matter how many promises God has made, they are 'Yes' in Christ."
Build Your Faith	*Romans 10:17* – "Faith comes by hearing, and hearing through the word of Christ."

KEEP IN TOUCH

Platform	Handle/Contact Info
YouTube	@RechargeYourFaith
TikTok	@lynn_r_davis @tokaboutquotes
Email	Lynnrdavisauthor@gmail.com
Blogger	Lynnrdavis.blogspot.com